Introduction

The original purpose of this book was to remind my family and close friends of my life in Germany between 1930 and 1939 and particularly during the pogrom (known generally as Kristallnacht) of 10 November 1938.

After I sent the manuscript of these German experiences to my good friend Walter Jaegle in Buchen, Germany, he immediately suggested it should be published in German to be disseminated among the local population of my home town to remind them of the ill-treatment of Jews in Germany during the Nazi era.

I then decided to write about my life in England during the second world war and my six year stay in Southern Rhodesia (now Zimbabwe) and sent these to Walter Jaegle as well. As a result (and with my agreement), Walter, together with Dr. Isabell Arnstein arranged for the book to be translated into German and published locally in two small volumes. I titled these two volumes "Exodus x 3" as they covered my life in Germany before WW2 up to exodus 1 to England, my schooldays in England during WW2 up to exodus 2 to Southern Rhodesia, and my six year stay with my parents in Bulawayo until exodus 3, my return to England.

This original English version covers these three parts of my life, each of which was shaped by political events that can be attributed directly or indirectly to the odious National Socialist regime in Germany.

Albert Lester
2023

Exodus x 3

A Memoir

Albert Lester

ISBN 978-1-915787-86-6

Printed in Great Britain by
Biddles Books Limited, King's Lynn, Norfolk

Exodus x3

I came into this world a few months after my grandfather died, an event that deeply affected my mother. People who believe in pre-natal influence maintain that her grief was transmitted to me while still in her womb because, so I was told later, I cried a lot as a baby and have, according to my wife, a melancholic and cynical attitude to life even now. Of-course, none of this is true. I am perfectly normal, — I think. It was not surprising therefore that following Jewish tradition, I was named after my grandfather Abraham, but this was Germanised to Albrecht, a name often associated with the German aristocracy. For good measure and for reasons unknown, my parents added two more names, Helmut and Julius.

Buchen

I was born and grew up in the small market town of Buchen (which means Beeches) in the Odenwald, (which means forest of Odin). The town, like many others in this part of the medieval world, was originally built like a fortress with high walls and a gate tower which still guards the entrance to the Marktstraße and the inner town. Every type of shop to meet the needs of the burghers of Buchen could be found in the Marktstraße, including our family business. Life on the street was peaceful and the shopkeepers generally got on well with each other. However, their animals did not. The street boasted two butcher shops which collected their meat from the slaughter house by dog cart hauled by two huge mastiffs. Every now and then the dogs from the two butchers met, resulting in a bloody dog fight which could only be stopped by nearby shopkeepers throwing buckets of cold water over the fighting animals.

The Marktstrasse

There were four other Jewish shops in the Marktsraße, one of which was a hardware store belonging to a colourful character called Jakob Bär. Every two or three days, Jakob would travel to the surrounding villages with his horse and buggy selling or delivering items needed by the farmers. After his rounds, he would return home via about a dozen hostelries where he refreshed himself. However on many occasions he would be so intoxicated after the first two or three stops, that the rest of the journey home was entirely in the hands (or hoofs) of his clever horse, who stopped at every bar he normally visited until he received a slap on the rump by the landlord, which told him to move on. Jakob would then arrive outside his house in such a state of inebriation that his wife would have to lift him off the buggy. She then led the horse to the barn where the buggy was unhitched and gave him another slap that made him trot through the town to his stable where a stablehand bedded him down. On one occasion I was present when the horse was unhitched and I was allowed to ride him back to the stable without a saddle or reins, holding onto his long mane.

After the rise of Hitler, Jakob's predilection to alcohol landed him in jail for couple of days. He was drinking in this favourite bar reading the official Nazi organ "Der Völkischer Beobachter" The logo of this paper was the German eagle holding a swastika. Jakob, in his half drunken state doodled over the logo. This "desecration" of the Nazi symbol was noticed by a neighbouring drinker, who reported him to the authorities. His crime was "Parteibeleidigung" or Party insult.

The town symbol is a prostrate naked boy who, it was said, was placed, backside outwards, on the town wall by a near starving population to show a besieging army that they still had enough food to bake a huge bun. As a result the attackers withdrew, and to commemorate this survival, a stone statue of the naked boy, called the Blecker, is paraded round the town on a cart every day during the Fastnacht (Carnival) period, and everyone in the street at the time is virtually forced by attendants in colourful costumes to kiss the Blecker's backside. Many people, including me, found the practice of kissing this stone posterior, where hundreds before me had put their lips, both abhorrent and positively unhygienic, so whenever I heard the cart coming, I either ran home or escaped into a side street.

The Blecker

During the Fastnacht period, I attended children's parades and parties, and was particularly proud of my jockey outfit, complete with cap and whip. I would walk through town to show it off, slapping the whip against my thighs. Later, I was debarred from these communal activities, including visiting the new local swimming-pool. Heaven forbid that the water should be contaminated by a non-Arian.

Certainly my childhood was a happy one until the early 1930s, when a certain Adolf Hitler made his presence felt and effectively ruined my father's business. Our extended family, consisting of my parents, sister, grandmother and maiden aunt literally lived above the shop which was on the ground floor of a large rambling three-storey house with two living rooms, seven bedrooms, kitchen, laundry room and an enormous area for drying clothes, storing all kinds of paraphernalia, trunks and hundreds of toys including two swings. Above the garage, attached to the house, was another storage area for firewood and more junk. My sister Hella, who is 4 years older and I slept in adjacent beds in a room separated from my parent's bedroom by a heavy curtain. Before going to sleep we would impersonate some of the inhabitants in our street including an old lady, Frau Künkel, who had a stammer. Because I had a slight stutter when I became exited, I was always bullied into mimicking her.

Despite this nightly humiliation, Hella and I got on well, although once she had learnt how to read she would immerse herself in a book and tell me to get lost whenever I wanted to play with her.

In the evenings we would listen to the radio or play records on a gramophone which had a huge trumpet-like speaker that resembled the logo of His Masters Voice, but without the dog. Sometimes we made music ourselves. My aunt played the piano, my mother the guitar and I completed the trio with my mouthorgan. The mouthorgan was replaced several times as a "payment" for sitting as a model for a friend of my mother, Ludwig Schwerin, who became famous in Berlin as a portrait painter of celebrities like Selma Lagerlöf, Thomas Mann, Stefan Zweig, Albert Einstein, Walter Rathenau, Ludwig Quidd and others. He later emigrated to Israel where he also painted David Ben-Gurion, but became better known for his wonderful landscapes of his new home.

My sister Hella and I

In the outfitters shop, which, with the necessary store rooms stretched for the full length of the house, one could buy all the goods required to clothe and shod a man or woman from underwear to overcoat. The business also included a small Bank and the Norddeutsche Lloyd travel agency with whose help the newly outfitted person could, as advertised by a large poster in one of the shop windows, enjoy a cruise to the Canaries, or the Americas. The same shop window also contained a wonderful 5 foot model of the liner "Columbus" which was greatly admired by all the children in the neighbourhood, especially when it was lit up at night.

My father, Herbert Levi, who had married into the business started by my grandfather Abraham Wolf, threw himself into the social life of the little town by joining the Voluntary Fire Service, heading the "Turnverein" or physical training club and being a member of a First Aid team. On one occasion he resuscitated a teenaged boy who had been electrocuted by a damaged cable in a workshop and whose heart had actually stopped. However, these efforts to integrate into the local community did not compare with the contributions to local life made by my so-called uncle, one Jakob Mayer, who lived diagonally opposite us in the Marktstrasse and who neglected his business by devoting nearly all his time to the social life of Buchen. He wrote poetry in the vernacular, composed songs which are still sung today, and was an active member of numerous local societies and clubs. He loved walking in the dense beech and oak forests surrounding the town and I fondly remember

Boy with mouthorgan. Painting by Ludwig Schwerin

Our house in the Marktsrasse

accompanying him on these walks on which he described and explained the medicinal and other properties of the numerous trees, shrubs, flowers and even mushrooms. Being a bachelor, he had his main meal at lunchtime prepared by the towns premier hotel, the Prinz Carl, and my sister and I had the unenviable task during the school holidays to collect his meal in a tiered food carrier from the hotel kitchen and then, to stop it getting cold, running down the Marktstrasse and up three flights of stairs to his flat.

The population of Buchen was mainly Catholic and until 1930 there was little or no friction or antagonism between the Christian and Jewish families. True, there was always a shadow of anti-semitism in Germany, but by and large it did not manifest itself in the Odenwald towns and villages. My sister Hella and I went to the local Kindergarten and at the age of six, to the local primary school. Many of the children from the neighbourhood came to play in our huge play area at the back of the house. My parents' best friends were non-Jewish as were my own close friends, Hans Baüerlein, Rudi Vollmer and Karl-Heinz Gehrig.

During the summer or autumn afternoons after school, the three of us would wander up to the Wartturm, an old 15th century 30 feet high sandstone watchtower, built by the burghers of Buchen to warn them of any advancing armies led by robber barons who roamed the countryside of what is now called Baden/Württemberg. On the way up to the tower, we would refresh ourselves by digging up a few sugar beet from the surrounding fields and cutting them into succulent slices with our pocket knives, until we were chased off by the "Feldhüter" or field warden. The winding road to the top was cut into the hillside with steep banks on each side. In winter, following the first snow, this road became a favourite toboggan run for the whole town, with the embankments acting as steeply raked bends similar to an Olympic toboggan run.

Then in 1933 life changed quite abruptly. My first recollection of the New Order was when Hans and Rudi, who were happily pulling me along the street on my roller skates were castigated by a man for in effect being the minions of a Jew boy. At my elementary school, our class teacher, a benign old gentleman who had even taught my mother, was replaced by a young lady teacher, a Fräulein Hennig, who hailed from the nearby town of Walldürn. She was also a leader of the local BDM (Bund Deutscher Mädchen, or Association of German Girls). Shortly after her arrival, on a sunny Sunday afternoon my friends Hans and Rudi and I were playing on top of a water reservoir on the road to Walldürn, when we saw Fräulein Hennig walking by below. For some inexplicable and misguided reason we called down: "Dürner Schiffle", which is the name of a type of biscuit made in Walldürn. There was no reaction from her, but the following day the three of us were called out, and in front of the whole class had to march up and down in front of her half a dozen times, shout "Heil Hitler" and give the Nazi salute. This, we were told, is the way one greets a fellow German.

By 1934, the presence of the Nazi party became a fact of life. Swastika flags flew from nearly every house every time the SA (Sturm Abteilung) or SS (Schutz Staffel) marched through the streets singing blood curdling anti-Semitic songs such as "When the Jewish blood spurts from the knife, everything goes better". On one occasion, I was so terrified that I fled the house by the garage door and took refuge in the house of my friend Hans, who lived at the end of the little side street adjoining our house. There, his mother and sister comforted me with bread and margarine until the parade was over.

Of-course not every member of the Nazi Party was antisemitic. When my sister Hella suddenly became very ill, I was sent to fetch our house doctor, Dr. Händel. The receptionist at his surgery told me that Dr Händel was away, but his locum would come instead. The doctor who arrived very quickly was young and tall and wore a beige raincoat. This surprised me as it was not raining. Furthermore he kept it on while he was examining Hella. He correctly diagnosed her as having meningitis and I was quickly dispatched to get a rubber ice-bag at the chemist and the ice to fill it from the "Krone", the nearest Tavern. The doctor was still with us when I returned and only then did I notice that he was wearing black boots, the type worn by the SS. Now I understood why he wore the raincoat.

Esslingen

Within a year my sister and I had to leave the local school because of our religion and my parents had to make alternative arrangements to enable us to continue our education.

My sister was the first to leave home. She was fortunate enough to be sent to a marvellous Jewish boarding school in Herrlingen near Ulm. This liberal school was run on the English house system and was revolutionary in its methods. The teachers were called by their Christian names and were regarded more as friends than pedagogues. Every morning there was a run through the school's own woods, followed by PT on the sports field and then showers before a great breakfast of oatmeal in cocoa, fresh rolls and coffee. Little did we know that ten years later the school would become the home of Field-Marshal Erwin Rommel and the place where he committed suicide after he was found to be implicated in the failed bomb plot on Hitler's life. The long winding road leading to the school is now named after him, despite the fact that he was the first German general, if not the only one, who was also a member of the Nazi party.

Unfortunately I only experienced this life when I stayed at the school for a month when my own school in Esslingen had holidays.

My school in the town of Esslingen near Stuttgart was just about the opposite. Originally it was built as an orphanage for Jewish children in the State of Württemberg. Its patron was King Wilhelm of Württemberg and was appropriately called the Wilhelmspflege. (Wilhelms care home). The building was impressively situated several feet above the junction of two roads overlooking the old castle of Esslingen. The interior was almost palatial with wide sweeping staircases and mosaic-paved corridors whose parallel edge pattern made excellent race tracks for Schuco racing cars, modelled on the Mercedes Benz car driven by our hero Rudolph Caraciola. In fact some of us often walked all the way from Esslingen to Untertürkheim where the actual racing car was exhibited in a show room of the Mercedes Benz factory.

Wilhelmspfege Esslingen

Because of the need to provide schooling for displaced Jewish children of both sexes, it was converted into a secondary school. Following the tradition of a faith sponsored orphanage, it was run on strictly orthodox lines with the full service every morning and evening and long graces before and after every meal. Every Saturday (Sabbath) we had to make our way down hundreds of well-worn steps by the side of the castle to the town synagogue for an even longer service. The only item we were allowed to carry in our pockets was a handkerchief as carrying anything else was deemed to be work. During the various fast days, some of the more religious boys did not even brush their teeth in case they accidentally swallowed some water.

Going to the synagogue on Saturdays or the Jewish holidays one always ran the risk of being abused or even stoned by local boys. However, we were told that on no account should we throw the stones back. One just had to accept the fact that one was disliked.

Fortunately, apart from Dr. Rothschild, the head master, all the teaching staff were young and capable. One of them seemed to take a special liking to me, probably because both our Christian names were Albrecht. I only changed it to Albert when I came to England, because the Brits had difficulties in pronouncing the last three letters of my name.

Apart from Arithmetic, History and Geography we were taught German literature, Hebrew and English. I immediately took a particular liking to English and had no difficulty with the irregular verbs. Somehow I felt that this would be my future tongue. Some of the Jewish families in Buchen had already emigrated to the USA and Cuba and I knew that my parents were in touch with my Uncle Alfred, who had seen the light early and moved with his family to, what was then, Southern Rhodesia which was a British self-governing colony.

In 1938, with the help of my uncle, my father obtained a resident's visa to Southern Rhodesia provided he worked on a farm. My uncle, who appeared to have made good in a relatively short period of time, knew a Swiss chicken farmer near the town of Bulawayo, who agreed to take my father on as an assistant. In the few weeks before his departure my father bought a pile of books and teaching manuals about chicken farming and even, at the request of his new employer, a state-of-the-art chicken incubator. The plan was for him to get settled in Rhodesia before my mother, my sister and I could follow.

However, my mother must have become aware of the rapidly deteriorating conditions for Jews in Germany and contacted a number of agencies who arranged for children to be sent to England. As a result a guarantor was found for my sister while I was registered with an organisation which sent children to England in organised groups, now known as the Kindertransport. I was of-course unaware of these negotiations, believing that my next home would be in Africa.

Kristallnacht

On the 8th November 1938 my father visited me at the school to say goodbye before leaving for Rhodesia. As a farewell present he bought me the latest Schuco product - the "Schuco Kommando". This clever little car could be stopped or started by directing the blast of a whistle into the slats forming the car's roof. The front wheels could be steered by moving the fog light on the radiator grille left or right, and by pulling the rear bumper out the car could be reversed. When the reversing car hit an obstacle, the bumper was pushed back in and the car moved forward.

The following day I was alone in the common room separated from the corridor by a wall of frosted glass. I spent a happy time putting the little blue car through its paces, deliberately letting it crash backwards into the toy lockers to see whether it would then move forward as predicted. Suddenly I heard a rumbling, rushing sound from the corridor and saw, through the frosted glass, a mass of shapes moving rapidly along the corridor towards the dining room. I shoved my new car into my back pocket and opened the door to see what it was all about, only to be swept away by a torrent of screaming, crying children running into the dining room.

The swarm then ran down a metal spiral staircase into the kitchen and from there over the kitchen garden to a wooden fence erected on top of a ten-feet-high retaining wall preventing the property from falling onto the streets below. One by one, the children climbed over the fence and jumped down the wall. When my turn came I looked down in terror, but seeing an even smaller boy supporting himself by his fingertips before dropping the remaining few feet, I followed suit and landed safely on my feet on the footpath below.

There was little else to do but to follow the crowd. Most of the children ran down towards the town, while a few others ran in the opposite direction towards a small wood, I decided to join the small group making for the woods where we eventually stopped in a small clearing to get our breath back. There we stayed for about half an hour wondering what to do. I remember clutching my pocketknife with my right hand to give me courage, but completely forgot the little car I had hastily stuffed into my back pocket. Clearly we could not stay there for ever, so, on the assumption that a girl would be less likely to be harmed than a boy, we persuaded the only girl in the party to make her way back to the school on a reconnaissance mission to find out what was going on.

Ten minutes later she returned and informed us that we were all to return to the school to receive further instructions. Slowly we trudged back down the road to the main entrance of the school past rows of non-uniformed men holding a variety of wooden clubs. I dared not look at their faces for fear of some violent reaction, but meekly climbed the few steps to the ornate entrance door which was partially smashed and dangling on its hinges. The floor inside was covered in broken glass, and a marble statue of Moses, a smaller replica of Michelangelo's masterpiece, had its head knocked clean off. What struck me was that all the lower octagonal panels of the doors to the classrooms had been neatly kicked in.

We filed past more sullen looking men and were herded into one of the classrooms. There we sat, about forty to fifty terrified boys and girls, too shocked to cry and too frightened to speak. I looked at the hole in the bottom of the door and really thought that the next stage would be a machine gun being poked through the opening and gunning us down.

After about five minutes, the door opened and Dr. Rothschild slowly walked in and sat down at the teacher's desk. He then put his head into his hands and quietly wept. The sight of this kindly old man breaking down in front of us opened the floodgates and everyone in that classroom burst into tears. None of the teachers were to be seen. I learnt later that they had all, like hundreds of Jews in Southern Germany, including my father, been sent to the Dachau concentration camp near Munich.

We waited, expecting worse to come, but after about another half hour of fear and trepidation, a woman came into the room and told us that we would all be moved to various families in Stuttgart while arrangements were made for us to travel home.

Word had got around the Jewish community that the school had been raided on what was later to be called Kristallnacht (night of broken glass) and many Jewish families rallied round to give the stricken children some temporary safe haven.

When my name was called out by the woman, I was told to pack whatever I could into one suitcase and wait in the common room. Eventually a lady arrived, took me by the hand and led me to a waiting car for the short journey to Stuttgart. I discovered that my hosts were both doctors, who were mercifully not molested by the thugs allegedly spontaneously expressing the clearly orchestrated Volkswut (people's anger) following the assassination of a minor diplomat in Paris by a Polish Jewish youth.

I stayed with this family for two fretful days until someone at my home could be contacted. I was given a train ticket from Stuttgart to Buchen which was a journey I normally had to make when I spent the vacation at home, but it meant travelling on my own and changing trains at Stuttgart, Heilbronn, Osterburken, and Seckach. On this occasion I had just settled down alone in the compartment in Stuttgart when I was joined by a man in an SS uniform with the menacing silver skull badge on his cap. Although he hardly noticed me, the very sight of this black uniform sitting opposite me filled me with terror and I only relaxed when he mercifully left the train at Heilbronn.

As it was, my father was arrested on the station in Stuttgart and despatched to Dachau, while my mother, who suspected what had happened, travelled to the Gestapo office in Karlsruhe to plead for his release on the grounds of him having his emigration papers and boat ticket to South Africa. She told me later how she flung my father's WW1 medals on the desk of the Gestapo officer and asked him whether this is how one rewards a war hero who had been seriously wounded at the front. Whatever the reason, she was successful in obtaining his release, providing he did not return home but travelled straight to Hamburg to board his ship. My mother then took a train to Hamburg to bid him farewell, so that when I arrived home I only found my aunt and grandmother to meet me. They were thankfully unharmed because they had locked themselves in, but Uncle Jakob, for all his good social works, was badly beaten up by the very people he had devoted his life to. Eight months later after my mother had wound up our affairs and left to join my father in Rhodesia, he committed suicide in his flat.

For the next month I stayed at home constructing cranes and bridges with my Märklin (the German equivalent of Meccano) set, which I increased in size over the years at Esslingen by swapping boring items such as gloves, pens and other toys for Märklin parts. These I then sent home (receiver paid) to my father who made wooden partitioned boxes for the different components. I also spent many hours playing with my model railways, whose locomotives and carriages were literally hand made by my two older cousins, one of whom, Fritz, was studying to be an engineer in Karlsruhe. He and his brother Heinz, who was at Heidelberg studying Drama, often stayed with us during their holidays. Both were railway enthusiasts and must have spent hours building these locomotives which were replicas of real railway engines. I hero-worshipped Fritz and was sure that one day I too would be an engineer. My parents encouraged my ambitions by buying me electric and clockwork motors for my Märklin set as well as a small collection of tools which my mother bitterly regretted when she discovered that I took it upon me to sharpen a set of ebony handled fruit knives with a newly acquired grindstone which left deep, ugly scratches across the polished stainless steel blades.

England

In January 1939 we were told that the school had been given permission to reopen, so I returned to carry on with my education. At the beginning of March 1939 the wife of the headmaster came into our classroom in the middle of a lesson and said I should quickly pack my belongings because I was being sent to England. I packed my suitcase, said good-bye to my friends and teachers, and two hours later was on the first stage of my journey home which involved the familiar four changes of trains. After I got home, the most important thing I had to do was to get some official travel documents, without which I could not have left the country. As I was too young to obtain a passport, I was issued with a "Kinderausweis" (Children identity pass).

The official at the "Landratsamt", the office which issued this document, was a particularly ardent Nazi called Allgeuer, who, apart from giving me the new statutory name of Israel, which was imposed on all Jewish males in 1938, decided on his own volition and for good measure to change my third name from Julius to Judas. I noticed the change when I had to sign the Kinderausweis but I said nothing. When you are eleven years old and Jewish, you don't mess with authority . I just wanted to get out. Out of this man's office, out of Buchen, out of Germany. From now on my name was Albrecht, Helmut, Judas, Israel Levi. No mistaking now that I was Jewish! The date was 17. March 1939.

Kinderausweis

A few days later my mother took me to the railway station in Karlsruhe, where I was put, together with a dozen other children, on the express train to Hamburg. Although my departure must have been traumatic for my mother, I only felt elation in the knowledge that I would be leaving the pain, indignities and humiliations of Germany for good.

In Hamburg, on the 21. March 1939, we boarded the United States Lines luxury liner "Manhattan" which, after an overnight stay in Le Havre, disembarked us three days later in Southampton. While on board we were formed into groups of about 20 children. Each group had a group leader known as a Madrich, who kept an eye on us and did his best to answer the many questions thrown at him. These leaders were generally young men and women who did an excellent job in keeping up our spirits.

After disembarking at Southampton we were put on a special boat train to Waterloo station in London. On the train one of the group leaders decided to teach us some basic English phrases and the British National Anthem, but for some inexplicable reason, he taught us to sing "God save the Queen"

S.S. Manhattan

although at the time Great Britain was ruled by King George VI. By the time we reached Waterloo we could sing the anthem and knew enough English to make polite replies including the peculiar convention of answering "How do you do" with "How do you do" back.

From the station platform we were led to the entrance of the Underground where I had my first experience of travelling on an escalator. However, we did not get as far as the tube train; instead we were marched into some unused access tunnels which became a holding area until our various hosts arrived to pick us up. Coming up from the Underground, I saw my first English Bobby. He looked at me, flipped my chin and smiled. I was stunned. Never had a policeman smiled at me before. I realized then what freedom meant.

After a few minutes I and half a dozen other boys were shepherded across the station forecourt by a young lady and onto a waiting school bus from Gayhurst School, a prep school in Gerrards Cross, Buckinghamshire. When we were safely seated, the bus trundled off across the Thames at Waterloo Bridge, down the Strand, up Whitehall, past Hyde Park and on to the old A40 to Gerrards Cross. The lady, who accompanied us, explained all the sights as we passed them in perfect German. Seeing London like this from the comfort of a small bus was absolutely enthralling and exciting.

Eventually we arrived at the Gayhurst School, where we were first met by the headmaster, Mr Gibbs, who, we learnt later, was on the committee which set up the small boarding school, specially created for refugee children like me. At Gayhurst we had our first English tea and cucumber sandwiches, were shown around the classrooms and sports fields by a pupil called Wolfgang, who was himself a refugee boy, but was by now bilingual. We were really made to feel welcome and I was quite sad to have to board the bus again to take us to our final destination "Woodside", our new school in Loudwater, near High Wycombe, Buckinghamshire.

Woodside

The school was originally a very large family house with 6 bedrooms, four reception rooms, an impressive entrance hall and a huge garden with two lawns, an enormous vegetable garden, and a grassy field big enough to cover two football pitches. A garage block with a loft was at the end of the wide curved driveway leading to the house. The bedrooms were converted into dormitories and the reception rooms into classrooms. The hall became the dining room at the centre of which was a long dark antiqued oak dining table. The boys sat on benches at each side and the headmaster Mr. Bolton and his wife presided from equally old looking leather backed armchairs at each end. Mr. Bolton was referred to as "Sir" and his wife as "Auntie". This reminded me of the school in Esslingen, where, because it was originally an orphanage, we called the headmaster's wife "Frau Mutter" (Mrs Mother). I suppose in the eyes of our new hosts we were all orphans.

The food was pretty good but it took me some time to get used to tea with milk. In Germany we only drank tea, perhaps with lemon, when we were ill. To my great delight we each received 6 pence a week pocket money, which we were urged to save until we were old enough to go to the cinema by ourselves.

Our teachers (some of whom lived in the school) were a varied bunch. Mathematics and Science was taught by Dr. Friedmann, a rather stern lady who was a university professor from Vienna. Dr. Braun, a Jewish judge from Berlin, who emigrated to England with his blonde German wife and young son, taught us Latin, while English, geography and history were taught by Mr. Bolton. A very attractive young lady teacher who arrived three days a week in a blue Morris Minor convertible, in which we all wanted a ride, read us English stories, presumably to help us with our pronunciation.

Having spent several years at a religious boarding school, with all the restrictions and taboos associated with clericalism, I found Woodside a breath of fresh air. However, we had to say grace before every meal and Sir muttered a few words of thanks at its end.

A month later, in April 1939, my sister Hella, arrived in England, thanks to the generosity and kindness of her guarantor, Maud Jellinek, a wealthy widow whose propensity to help other people seemed to have no bounds. Her large and beautiful house in Gerrards Cross was always full of refugees from various European countries occupied by Germany before the war. Even her cook and housekeepers were middle class ladies only too happy to accept more menial positions in order to satisfy British Visa requirements and thus escape persecution. Then in June, the same year my mother, having sold our house at a knock-down price and packed up what she could in several containers, travelled on the liner "Pretoria", the same ship that my father had used, to Cape town and thence to Bulawayo, Southern Rhodesia to join him. The containers followed on a slower freighter called the "Usukuma", which was so slow that by the time it reached the South Atlantic, war had broken out. The ship was spotted by a British warship off the coast of what is now Namibia, and promptly scuttled herself. When my sister told me about this, I was sorry but could not feel strongly about losing our bedding and pots and pans. Then she pointed out that the losses also included my huge Meccano set. That really floored me. Why couldn't they have waited a few days longer before going to war and allowed the ship to reach Cape Town?

The Boltons went to the local C of E church in Loudwater every Sunday and after a few weeks we were invited to join them. However, before we could actually go, those of us who could still contact their parents, had to obtain their permission. I duly wrote to my parents in Rhodesia and explained that I was quite interested to see how other people pray to their god and promptly got their consent. The next Sunday about twenty of us trooped off to church under the watchful eye of Auntie. Having been cured of any religious fervour by the forced participation of Jewish services and rituals while at Esslingen, I was not impressed by neither the stark interior of the village church nor the boring and uninspiring C of E service. The following Sunday after breakfast, those of us who had attended church the previous Sunday were asked to get ready for church. I and two or three other boys felt that we had seen enough to satisfy our curiosity and expressed our wish to stay at home.

This did not please Auntie. Our parents had given permission and this was interpreted as an order to attend. An argument started, Sir was summoned and as they could hardly frogmarch us to church under escort, we were told, that provided we learnt several chosen psalms by heart while the others were in church, we could stay away from the holy edifice. After ten weeks this punishment was lifted, during which time I learnt some twenty psalms, but we were spared the dreaded Psalm 119, the longest in the book. Today, the only one I remember is Psalm 23.

After about a year, the Jewish community in High Wycombe got wind that some boys at Woodside had been persuaded to attend church, an act regarded by them as a first step towards conversion to Christianity. On the basis that everybody should at follow at least one religion, Mr. Bolton must have struck a deal with them, because only the abstainers like me were strongly advised to attend a special Jewish children's service and religious education session every Saturday morning, hastily and paradoxically set up in the Friends' Meeting House in High Wycombe. This I found to be even more objectionable than the church, mainly because it meant a two mile walk to and from the place, rain or shine. Knowing that I would never be forced to continue with these indoctrinations, I simply stayed away. Having lived so long in the the religious environment of Esslingen, I was left with a firm belief that there was a higher power, who I was sure would protect me provided I was "good" and honest. On the other hand, I was equally convinced that this had nothing to do with the rituals, taboos and dogmas followed by both of the religions I was asked to accept.

One example of honesty being rewarded centred round the little pocket knife that I had clutched so vehemently when we sat in the little wood after Kristallnacht. Although I always had it in my right hand trouser pocket, I did manage to lose it, possibly while playing football in the field behind the house. A long and tedious search of the field and the grounds, the classrooms and dormitories proved to be futile. However, on one of the lawns, I did find a shiny pair of chromium plated nail clippers, which I new belonged to a boy in our dormitory. On the principle of "finders keepers" I kept it hidden in my drawer in the room. A few days later I found one of the boys handling what I was convinced, was my knife. When I approached him and demanded it back, he declared that it was given to him by his aunt. I realised that this type of knife was hardly unique and reluctantly accepted his explanation. Then for some inexplicable reason, I realised that hiding the nail clippers in my drawer made no sense, as I did not dare to use them openly. I therefore handed them over to the rightful owner, saying that I had just found them. He was overjoyed at getting them back. A day later, the boy who found my knife gave it back to me with some feeble excuse that he got the knives muddled up. I still have the knife, albeit a little battered, displayed in my memento cabinet, a reminder that honesty pays!

War

A few doors away lived an English couple called Brown, who sometimes invited me and another boy to spend Sundays with them and their teenage son Donald, who was waiting to be called up for military service. I remember being on their well kept lawn looking for four- leaf-clovers when I was called into the house to listen to the wireless. It was 11.15 am on the 3rd September 1939, and the speaker on the air was Mr. Neville Chamberlain. Germany had attacked Poland the day before and he had asked Germany for an undertaking to withdraw their troops. At the end of his short speech, he said: "I have to tell you that no such undertaking has been received and that consequently this country is at war with Germany." The Browns looked shocked and frightened, but I felt glad. Glad that at last the hated Nazi regime in Germany would be attacked and destroyed. In my innocence, I never had any doubt that this would happen, even during the darkest days of the war when everyone expected a German invasion. Two years later Donald, who joined the RAF, was killed.

I had always considered my stay in England to be a temporary one, because my real objective was to rejoin my parents in their new home in Southern Rhodesia. Indeed, on two occasions my sister and I were asked to pack our bags for our journey to Africa, but on both occasions, as we were waiting for the boat train at Waterloo and later at Euston Station, we heard that our journey had been cancelled because of enemy action in Southampton and Liverpool respectively. As a farewell present for the first abortive journey, Auntie presented me with a leather bound copy of the Bible and made me promise to read one chapter every day. I have kept the bible, but alas, not the promise.

Soon after war was declared, our cellar at Woodside became an air raid shelter and we were all provided with gas masks. However, life went on as before and by October 1939, we were all considered to be proficient enough in English to be sent to the local schools. Some of the boys went to the local elementary school in Loudwater while others, including me, attended a school evacuated from West London and housed in a large wooden British Legion building in Wycombe Marsh. As all the children were in effect new to the area, we German boys were not very different to them, refugees from German action. I got on famously with most of my classmates, swapping stamps and cigarette cards and when, on the only occasion I can remember, one boy called me Bloody German, another quickly intervened and said that I was one of the Good Germans. A few months later, all the classes moved to a brand new school building, called Hatters Lane Senior School, a few miles away, with the latest sports and classroom facilities. What I do remember mostly about this school is our class Master, Mr. Ripley. Every morning started with assembly and prayers in the well equipped gymnasium. However, this was not sufficient for Mr. Ripley, who, being a member of the Plymouth Brethren, decided that the assembly prayers were too shallow and had therefore to be augmented by further prayers in the classroom. He would screw up his eyes, raise his head to heaven and tightly clasp his hands in supplication, while he prayed for us, the school, our soldiers, sailors and airmen and of-course victory. He firmly believed every word of the Bible and told us countless times that when other religious sects called at his house to deliver pamphlets extolling their particular brand of christianity, he would cut them short by brandishing the Bible in his right hand with the words: "Why should I use a candle when I have the sun".

Although my English was good enough to enable me to participate in all class activities, there were occasions when I was confused by similar words having different meanings. Sir had a terrier called Kim and I loved playing with him. One day I wanted to take Kim for a walk, so I knocked on the door of the headmaster's sitting room where he was entertaining a few guests and was met with howls of laughter when I asked him whether I could "become" the dog to take him for a walk. (in German "bekommen" means to get)

One day we were called into the hall at Woodside to be introduced to a tall, stout gentleman in a brown uniform, short trousers and a large hat, the local scout master. He explained to us the advantages and benefits of scouting, and the following week some of us attended our first scout meeting at the local church hall. Unfortunately the committee looking after us could not justify the cost of kitting us out in proper scout uniforms, so I did the best I could by wearing shorts and getting matron to sew my tenderfoot badge on one of my shirts. I enjoyed the sing-songs and talks on field craft and even the rough and tumble of British Bulldog, but could have easily done without the opening prayers.

The following year, all the Woodside boys in the Boy Scouts spent two exciting weeks under canvas with the Berkhamstead scout troop in Sussex and learnt how to carry an axe safely, make a fire with no more than two matches, and use no more than three sheets of loo paper; all useful stuff for surviving in the wilds of Sussex.

Stokenchurch

Over the next two years, more and more boys left to live with relatives or their benefactors who usually sent them to more prestigious schools, with the result that a decision was made in the summer of 1941 to close Woodside down. We now became the responsibility of the Refugee Children's Movement, generally known by their address in London, Bloomsbury House. Arrangements were made to place the remaining boys, singly or in pairs with various foster parents. So it came about that another boy, Emil Stein, whose parents were unable to leave Berlin, and I were billeted with a Miss Newlands, an evacuated teacher from West Kensington, who lived with her bedridden mother in a cottage behind the Red Lion public house in the village of Stokenchurch, between HighWycombe and Oxford. Predictably the place was called Red Lion Cottage.

From time to time I stayed a few days with my sister, who shared a flat with two other girls in Lexham Gardens, Kensington. During one of these visits I experienced what it was like to be in London during an air raid. I was already in bed when the air raid warnings sounded, so I got up and put on my dressing gown ready to go downstairs to a makeshift shelter under the stairs on the ground floor. However, when I knocked on my sister's door to alert her, she simply told me to go back to bed. The other girls seemed equally unconcerned. Ten minutes later after I had returned to bed, I heard the whistle of the bombs and the bangs of the anti-aircraft guns in Hyde Park opening up. I lay there, terrified, itching to go down to the shelter, but as the girls, who were used to the nightly raids, showed no fear, I as a "man" had to follow their example and stick it out.

As the war progressed I became really frightened as the German army occupied more and more of Europe. However, everything changed on my birthday. On the 23. October 1942 Montgomery defeated Rommel at the battle of El-Alamein, after which the Germans lost North Africa, Sicily, Italy, France and in effect the war. As Winston Churchill put it: "Now this is not the end. It is not even the beginning of the end. But it is, perhaps, the end of the beginning."

For a short while Emil and I attended the local village school, whose headmaster could have come out of a Dickens novel. The arithmetic lesson was always a nightmare. Although neither Emil nor I were ever touched, children were caned when they got their sums wrong. Another boy who just could not keep up in class was sent out to look after the headmaster's garden. When we told Miss Newlands about the conditions, she, to her credit, managed to persuade the local education authorities to find both of us a place at the Shoreditch Technical School which had been evacuated from London and was housed in some outbuildings of the local Technical School. As I had always wanted to become an engineer, this was a dream come true. Despite some nasty rows and arguments I had with Miss Newlands, I will be eternally grateful for her efforts to secure us a better education.

Across the road from the new school in High Wycombe was the "Mead", a large grassy area used occasionally as a fairground and for special celebratory events such as War Weapons Week or Wings for Victory Week. Along one edge of the Mead ran a small slow- flowing brook which was wide enough to act as a boating lake. During our lunch break, I sometimes took a boat out and rowed for half an hour to build up my puny muscles. One sunny day, I was in the middle of the lake when I heard an aircraft engine which sounded weird. I could tell the difference between a British and German bomber by the throb of the engines, but this was different. When I looked up I saw what it was. A V1, the German pilotless flying bomb nicknamed the Doodlebug, which was probably meant to hit London, but clearly had a serious navigational malfunction. My immediate reaction was to row for the shore, as one was supposed to throw oneself on the ground as soon as the engine cut out. It then took a few seconds for the bomb to hit the ground. By the time I reached the bank of the pond, it had passed, travelling over the town to open country. The next day we heard that it crashed on the edge of a children's playground in a village called Fingest, where my sister was at the time working as a land girl. She actually helped to bandage up some of the children who were hurt, but as it was lunchtime most of the children had gone home to eat, and the ones who were there were miraculously on the other side of the playground.

The Yanks are coming

A few months after the Japanese attack on Pearl Harbour in early December 1941, we saw our first American soldier. In fact, he was probably an airman, because the American 8th Airforce had taken over the prestigious Wycombe Abbey Girls Public School, which we passed every time we went to our sports grounds. Now, as we passed the familiar gates, we saw the American sentries with their white helmets and wooden truncheons. I was dying to see inside the high walls surrounding the school, and a few weeks later my wish was granted. As a gesture of pan-Atlantic friendship, my class was invited to watch an American Football match at the new camp. What struck me most were:

a)   The gravel paths had been replaced by concrete roads on which rolled a constant stream of trucks and Jeeps, and

b)   Lined up in a neat row outside the football pitch were four Service ambulances.

When I saw how the players charged and bashed each other, I understood why they were there.

Another manifestation of the American "occupation" was the appearance at school of the V Pack. This should more correctly have been called a VD Pack, for in its paper wrapper were two condoms on which the words "Against VD" were stamped, two tubes of cream and a set of instructions printed on thin grease-proof paper. How these packs appeared was a mystery. The most popular speculation was that it was brought to school by a boy whose older sister knew an American. What struck me was that the printed words were "Against VD" and not "Against pregnancy"! An interesting choice of priorities by the US military.

Wycombe Technical School

In the spring of 1943 when the air raids on London had almost stopped due to Hitler's concentration on his war in Russia, the school moved back to Shoreditch in London, and Emil and I were transferred to the Wycombe

Technical School. I loved the new school. I looked forward to the science and maths classes and even enjoyed the non-technical lessons like English, geography and history. Miss Everton, our English teacher, took a particular liking to Emil and me and invited us to her house for tea. When I was in hospital following a double mastoid operation she travelled all the way to Oxford to keep me supplied with books, many of which had the familiar red cover of Victor Golantz's Left Book Club. She was as open about her support for Labour as Miss Thomas, our History teacher was about her loyalty to the Liberals. As my parents now lived in a British colony, I was particularly interested in the opinions of the Left on colonialism.

The new school boasted a woodworking and a metalworking workshop. Attendance at both was compulsory, but I always considered the metal workshop to be the more relevant to my plans for the future, although I quite enjoyed making an oak coffee table, some oak book ends and a laboriously hand-carved walnut fruit bowl which I presented to Auntie Maud. She was so delighted with them that on one of my birthdays she gave me a huge lockable wooden tool box containing every kind of woodworking tool one could think of, saws, drill brace, chisels, mallet, hammers, wood plane, pliers, the lot.

However, it was during a woodworking class that my hope of becoming a prefect was dashed. Another boy had "borrowed" a newly sharpened chisel while my back was turned. It was not difficult to find the culprit, but when he refused to return it an argument turned into a scuffle. As fighting in a workshop was a grave offence, the master in charge immediately sent us to see the Mr. Davies, the headmaster whom he called the"Boss". After waiting a few minutes outside the Boss's door, he opened it, beckoned us in and promptly caned us on each hand. Only then did he ask us what we had done. By that time there was no point in explaining who had started the confrontation, so we just said : "fighting, Sir" and trooped out with a few silent curses and ten swollen fingers. The pain soon went away, but the indelible black mark on my record debarred me from ever being a prefect. Emil on the other hand, had no such blemish and was made a prefect in charge of the library.

Once a week was sports day and for the first time in my life I had to play cricket. I found this game to be both dangerous and time wasting.

Dangerous, because facing a very hard ball coming at you at a high speed was terrifying and time wasting, because I calculated that on average 95% of the time one did nothing. 50% of the time one was in the pavilion waiting for one's innings. The other 50% were on the field, but since I was usually asked to play long-stop, statistically only one in ten balls might come my way. Hence, I calculated that the time one spent just sitting or standing around was: 50% + (90% of 50%) = 95%. Needless to say, that with such enthusiasm I was never asked to bowl or keep wicket.

I only fared slightly better with football. I only managed to get into my class team because when the captain was deciding on who should be one of the half-backs, the sports master advised him to: "Take young Levi, he can't play much football but he does get in the way."

Farm holiday camp

During the summer holidays of 1943, I joined a group of teenage Jewish boys and girls for a working holiday in Bredons Norton, Worcestershire. The idea was to help farmers with the harvest, and I had pleasant visions of riding back from our work in the corn fields on top of a cart full of hay. Instead, we spent most of the day picking up stones from a field that seems to have grown them, putting them into a basket and depositing them on a huge pile at one end of the field. We slept in large camouflaged army tents on straw palliasses which we had to fill ourselves. Whether it was the palliasse or the backbreaking work in the fields, I seemed to drop off to sleep as soon as I hit the sack.

However, the evenings more than made up for the hard work during the day. After a healthy and hearty dinner we all gathered around a blazing camp fire and sang songs to the accompaniment of an accordion and a couple of guitars. I noticed that there was a distinct pairing up between some of the older boys and girls, and for the first time I felt the urge to copy them. Looking around, I noticed an attractive girl sitting by herself. Slowly and as unobtrusively as I could, I edged my way towards her and sat down beside her. To my joy and delight, she turned to me, smiled and asked me my name.

Farm holiday camp in Worcestershire

"Albert", I said, "What's yours"

"Ilse, Ilse Echt, actually its Ilse von Echt, but I dropped the von when I came to England"

"I never heard of a Jewish von" I said

"You have now" she replied.

I didn't pursue the point. May be only her mother was Jewish. Who knows.

Ten minutes later I copied the older boys and put my arm round her shoulders. As she snuggled closer my heart leapt. This surely must be love. Fortunately we were in the same working party, so we travelled together on the back of a lorry to and from work and took our meals together. Sadly, the two weeks just flew by after that and although we exchanged addresses and wrote a few letters to each other, we never met again. Nevertheless, after this experience this 15-year old boy looked at girls differently.

Oxford hospital

Ever since I was a young boy, I had had trouble with my ears. While other children had measles or chickenpox, I had ear ache. The remedy was Odalgan, a brand of ear drops which usually stopped the pain after a day. So when I developed an ear ache at the beginning of January 1944, the similar remedy was applied, but this time the pain was accompanied by a discharge. For two weeks, our house doctor, who was on Christian name terms with Miss Newlands, came every day to clean them out, until on the 20th January he decided I needed to see a specialist in Oxford. The following day, Miss Newlands took me to Oxford to see a Mr. MacBeth the senior ENT surgeon at the Radcliffe Infirmary, for what I thought would be another examination and clean-out. Within half an hour of seeing him, I was in a ward having the hair around my ears shaved off. I asked the nurse for the reason for this unusual procedure.

"You'r a lucky boy" she said, "you'r going to the theatre to-night"

"Oh yes", I said jokingly, "what am I going to see?"

"MacBeth" she said with a smile

An hour later I was on the operating table with Mr. Macbeth performing a mastoid operation on the right ear, while at the same time a Canadian army surgeon, seconded to the hospital, performed a similar procedure on the left. The next three weeks at the Radcliffe were really quite enjoyable. Being the only boy in a ward with grown ups, I was spoilt by the nurses who were all young and pretty. Everybody I knew came to visit me at some stage and brought me books and fruit. I got through 2 volumes of Greek mythology and a Left Book Club book brought by our English teacher, Miss Everson, a visit which really bucked me up. Miss Newlands visited me a number of times, as did Emil and Kurt, another ex Woodside boy who now lived in Oxford.

When my wounds had healed, the almoner decided that I needed to spend three weeks to recuperate. The chosen venue was St. Josephs Convalescent

Home in Bournemouth, a Catholic establishment run by kind, elderly, but rather bossy nuns, very different from the young cheerful nurses I had got used to.

The nurse who applied the last bandage before I embarked on my train journey to Bournemouth was aware that the trains would all be overcrowded, mainly with servicemen travelling to or from their camps. To ensure my getting a seat, she formed the bandages on my ear into a huge turban which worked a treat, because as soon as I got onto the train, one of the soldiers got up, offered me his place and lifted my only suitcase up on the luggage rack. At Reading, where I had to change trains, two soldiers almost lifted me up and deposited me on the platform with a: "Good luck, Abdul." On the next train I could not even get into a compartment and had to stand in the corridor for the rest of the way.

As at the Radcliffe, I was the youngest patient and was treated almost like a mascot by the mainly elderly residents. They took me on walks through the picturesque Bournemouth Chines telling me how they got their injuries or maladies that landed them at St. Joseph's. There was one younger convalescent called Joe, who walked with two sticks and had a permanently bent back. It turned out he was a young amateur boxer from the East End of London, who was virtually crippled by too many kidney punches. His advice to me at the time was: "Always look after yer kidneys, mate". This stayed with me and reminded me years later to always wear a kidney belt when I rode my motorbike. He also related stories of his sexual adventures before he was laid low by the kidney punches and gave me another invaluable piece of advice:

"When you want to get to know a bird at a party, always go for the best looker"

"Why" I asked

"You'll find out" he replied with a wink. I decided to take his advice, if I ever got the chance.

After four weeks at the convalescent home I went to Gerrards Cross to stay with Mrs. Jellinek, my sister's guarantor, known by everybody as Auntie

Maud, who decided to take me under her wing as well. All this was arranged without my knowledge. After two weeks with Auntie Maud, I returned to Stokenchurch and on 20 March I went back to school, having lost nearly a whole term. Sometimes during summer when the days were warm and sunny, we had our lessons outdoors in the school playground, and it was on such a day, that our lesson was disturbed by a a dozen fighter aircraft roaring noisily over our heads at such a low altitude that we could see the stripes painted on the underside of their wings. It was the 6th June 1944, our first visual evidence of the long awaited allied invasion of Europe. The day before, the Americans had entered Rome. The war was going well.

I had hoped that my ear problems had been finally resolved, but mid July, while I was spending another few days at Auntie Maud's in Gerrards Cross, I had again such a painful ear ache that her doctor was summoned who, after a thorough investigation, immediately arranged for me to be re-admitted to the Radcliffe in Oxford. There I underwent another two weeks of treatment until the infection had gone. Walking around the ward, I got particularly friendly with a soldier who had been evacuated from Normandy with serious injuries to his jaw, face and hands. Amazingly, unlike to-day's strict rules, he was allowed to smoke and I used to take his cigarettes out of their packet, placed them between his lips and lit them for him.

History repeated itself, for after the Radcliffe had done their bit, I was again dispatch to the St. Joseph's Convalescent Home in Bournemouth. This time I did not have a turban and I had to stand in the train corridor all the way. As I was still classified as an enemy alien, like on my previous visit, I had to report my arrival at the police station and obtained permission to stay for a few weeks. Clearly, as the allied operations in France were well underway, I was not considered a threat any more despite being in a position to see all the roads to the beach crammed with tanks, lorries, jeeps and other military hardware, ready to be shipped to Europe to support the troops.

Again, as before, after my stay at St. Joseph's I went back to Gerrards Cross, despite still having a slight but manageable discharge from my ears. This was evidently reported by the nuns in Bournmouth to the Radcliffe in Oxford, because in the first week of September 1944 I received a letter from the hospital asking me to return to them the next day for an operation on my nose because one ear, the one handled by Mr. MacBeth, refused to drain. The procedure to correct this, was carried out under a local anaesthetic which, though painless, enabled me to hear the crashing and banging as they bored a hole through the bone.

After another week in hospital I was sent to stay for a further week with a Mrs. Franklin-Kohn in Oxford, who, with her daughter Hele, showed me the sights and delights of Oxford, but what I remember most during this stay, was the sight of hundreds of bombers towing gliders making their way to what was soon to be announced as the massive (but subsequently ill-fated) airborne attack on Arnhem on 17 September 1944.

Holmer Green

I had now missed almost a whole term at school and was concerned about being able to catch up when I returned. Then I received a letter from a Mrs Jacobs from High Wycombe who worked for Bloomsbury House, the headquarters of the "Refugee Children's Movement," the organisation who were still responsible for us. This letter informed me that on the 21 September 1944, my new home would be with a Mr. & Mrs. Bruton, who lived in a village called Holmer Green between High Wycombe and Amersham. When I arrived at my new home a week later I was pleasantly surprised to find my friend Emil Stein already in residence.

The Brutons were a kindly working class family who clearly needed the money Bloomsbury House paid them for our keep. Mr. Bruton was a butcher's assistant and earned extra money by helping out in other people's gardens. Mrs. Bruton was a waitress in the café of the Palace cinema in High Wycombe. They worked hard to bring up their teenage daughter Josie, pay their mortgage and run their little Ford 10 motor car. On a non-rainy Sunday we would all "take the car for spin" and go to Windsor or Marlow to be by the river. Mrs Bruton was a chain smoker and introduced me to the weed by convincing me that if you didn't smoke, you were not a man. Not only did I start smoking cigarettes but also sported a pipe which resulted in my having permanently grotty jacket pockets from the spillage of a half-smoked pipe. I gave up what I soon learnt to be a very unhealthy habit, on the day my first son was born. After becoming a father, there was no need to give further proof of my manhood.

Every month Emil and I were invited for lunch by a George Kaufman who, with Mrs Jacobs must have been asked by Bloomsbury House to keep an eye on their charges in High Wycombe. He was a Civil Engineer who had evacuated himself from Victoria Street in London and had set up a small design office in his beautiful house in the best part of the town. He had a very attractive wife, an even more attractive 17 year old daughter June as well as a young son called Richard. Both Emil and I were secretly in love with June, but it was just a dream as her boy friend worked in Mr. Kaufman's office. When I left school Mr. Kaufman wrote a glowing testimonial for me which I used every time I applied for a job, but when years later I visited him to discuss my possible membership of the Association of Consulting Engineers he had forgotten about it.

In 1940, Robert Wagner, the Gauleiter of Baden in Germany, complied with the directive to permanently clear Germany of all Jews, by sending all the remaining Jews in his domain to a detention camp in Gurs, in the yet unoccupied Vichy France. Included in this transportation was my maiden aunt Marie, who was really my second mother when I was a child. She took me for walks, read me stories and probably had more to do with me than my mother, who was involved in the business and, in the later years, was frequently away from home.

While I was at Woodside I received a letter from her through the Red Cross, telling me of her predicament, including a request for a little money to enable her to buy some extra food. I showed the letter to Auntie Maud, who immediately arranged for some money to be transmitted to her via the Red Cross. Over the next year I received a few more letters all of which I answered within days. Then the letters stopped. Years later in the spring of 1945, I received a brown paper parcel from the Red Cross which contained all the letters I had sent her—unopened. The realisation that my aunt must have felt neglected, if not betrayed because I had not bothered to answer her letters, shook me to the core. I felt angry and vengeful. I decide to skip the next day's school, borrowed some money from Mrs. Bruton and took an early train to London. I assumed that there would be an Air Attache in London, because I knew that some Rhodesian pilots flew with the RAF, so I went to Rhodesia House in the Strand and asked to see the man in charge of the Rhodesian Air Force in the UK. My assumption was correct, for I was directed to an office where a bemused middle-aged Air Force officer asked me what I wanted.

I told him the story of my returned letters, that my parents lived In Southern Rhodesia, and ended with a fervent plea to be allowed to join the Rhodesian Air Force, so that I could avenge my aunt's pain and distress. I told him how I longed to get one of those hated swastikas into the sights of a Spitfire.

He listened sympathetically, smiled benignly, got up from his chair and put his hands on my shoulder.

"How old are you, son"

"Seventeen, Sir" I replied

"Go back to school and finish your studies. The war with Germany will soon be over"

I travelled back to High Wycombe dejected and with a feeling of utter helplessness.

Only after the war did I discover that after the Germans decided to occupy Vichy France in November 1942, all the inmates from Gurs, including my aunt, were transported to Auschwitz.

The prize

In the third year of school, most of the pupils in my class, 3A, worked a little harder than normal because the pupil with the highest aggregate marks in the end of term examination received a much sought after prize, a top of the range set of drawing instruments comprising two compasses with extension bars, dividers, spring compasses, a spin compass, draughting pen, the works.

My heart was set on winning these instruments and as each set of marks for the different subjects was read out after each test, I realised that I was well on the way to victory. There was only one exam left to be taken, Free Drawing. In this test we were asked to design a dust cover for a book entitled "To-day". Most of the class drew the latest aircraft or other technical marvel, but I decided that the book was a mystery novel and showed the slightly curled leaf of a pull-off calendar impaled by a dagger, with day 13 and "TO-DAY" instead of the name of the day. When the marks were read out, my name was not called. I jumped up and queried the omission to be told that I had not submitted a design. However, he said, there was a submission which was the most imaginative but was given zero marks because it bore no name or signature. I was absolutely shattered. This of-course seriously reduced my aggregate and I had to forgo my coveted prize. To this day I have not forgiven that art teacher.

Towards the end of our three year course, as the war in Europe was nearing its end, someone decided to form a South Buckinghamshire Youth Parliament. Elections were therefore held in every secondary school in the area to elect suitable candidates to represent them as members of this parliament, whose speaker was actually the deputy speaker of the House of Commons. The Tech. as it was known, could send two delegates and the half a dozen boys who had political aspirations had to set out and justify their policies to a full assembly of the school. Emil stood as a Conservative and I, possibly inspired by Miss Everton's reading matter, decided to represent my own brand which I named Democratic Socialist. Amazingly, after presenting our case to a cheering audience, in the school gymnasium, Emil and I, the only non-British candidates, polled the most votes and were duly elected to represent the school.

I attended two sessions of the parliament as a backbencher, because the Conservatives had the greatest number of members. However, soon after the second session I left school and High Wycombe and lost touch with the other people I knew.

After VE Day, the country had its first post war election. I was a very enthusiastic Labour supporter and actually did some house to house canvassing for them. I quite enjoyed this until one dear lady, recognising my German accent, told me to go back where I came from. From then on, I confined my activities to licking envelopes.

On the day the election results were announced, Emil and I went to a party at the house of a girl from the arts department who later became a well known BBC actress. One could tell from her polished accent that she had well heeled parents with a big house. A friend from school and I were glued to the wireless as the election results were read out, when a dear old lady came over to where we were sitting and asked us who was winning. 'Labour," I said triumphantly. "Ah well", she sighed,, "As long as these dreadful Socialists don't get in". I looked at my friend who gave me a very slight smile, but neither of us had the heart to disillusion her. That day, the country took a sharp left turn and waved Mr. Churchill good bye. He had won the war, but lost the peace.

End of school

During the last term, both Emil and I decided to sit the examination for the University of London Matriculation and I spent a few days with my sister in London whose flat was not far from Imperial College where the exams were held. On the day that America dropped the first nuclear bomb on Hiroshima, I received a letter telling me I had passed.

After our schooldays ended, Emil stayed on for another year to take his Inter-BSc, and won a scholarship to the LSE, but I was told by the powers-that-be at Bloomsbury House that arrangements were underway to return me to my parents in Rhodesia as soon as possible. They clearly wanted to clear their list of liabilities. In the meantime, because they were aware of my engineering ambitions, they would endeavour to find me a temporary position with an engineering company to get some practical experience in a design office. They also gave me a number of addresses of families in London who took in lodgers. I travelled to London and started with one in Blenheim

Crescent, North Kensington, because my sister's flat was not too far away in Marylebone Road. The lady, a Mrs. Kean, who came to the the door was so friendly, that after seeing the room and sharing a cup of tea, I agreed to her terms and moved in the following week.

Work and play

The next item on the agenda was to find a job. Again Bloomsbury House was helpful as usual and sent me the names of two employers who, predictably, were both refugees from Germany who had made good in this country. The first was a small company which designed food mixers. They offered me a job in their drawing office, but I felt that they really needed someone with more experience and had clearly overestimated my ability. I declined their offer for fear of letting them down.

The second company manufactured paper products such as toilet rolls, paper napkins, doilies and notebooks. They did however design and build their own very sophisticated production machines and I applied in writing to be a trainee draughtsman in their design department. A few days later I was invited to attend an interview at their office which, coincidentally and conveniently was in Westbourne Grove, within walking distance of my new home.

My appointment was with a Mr. Jacoby, the Chief Engineer, and I was shown into his unoccupied office to wait for him. A few minutes later an elderly gentleman came into the office and asked me who I was. I explained the reason for my visit, and noticing my German accent he asked me what part of Germany I came from. I told him I came from the Odenwald, but had gone to school in Esslingen. He then introduced himself as the Managing Director of the company, and told me that his nephew went to the same school. In fact, when he told me his name, I realised that his nephew actually had sat next to me in class. We then had a pleasant general chat about schools and work until the Chief Engineer arrived to interview me properly with the MD watching fro the other end of the room. I proudly showed Mr. Jacoby some of the engineering drawings I made at school of the more common engineering components. He seemed satisfied but then pointed to one drawing and asked me:

"Would you forge or cast this piece ?"

"Forge it". Wrong answer. Next:

"Where would you start machining it?" I pondered this a little while and then admitted

"Don't know, Sir"

This question and answer session went on for a while longer and things were not going at all well. Then suddenly the MD, who was watching me floundering and giving all the wrong answers, cut the interview short by saying:

"Mr. Jacoby, why are you asking this boy all these questions. He is clearly out of his depth, but it makes no difference because I have already decided to take him on."

That's how I landed my first job!

A week later I started work in their London office under the tutelage of a Mr. Weber, the Chief Draughtsman who was also a refugee from Germany and Mr. Duke, a mildly spoken design engineer who was everything I thought an engineer should be. He had just designed, drawn and detailed an ingenious new machine for threading wire spirals into note books, when the Chief Engineer told him that he could not spare any one in the workshop to build the prototype. Mr Duke then simply exchanged his white coat for a brown one, went into the workshop and made and assembled all the components for the complete machine himself. That, I decided, is what I want to be able to do as well.

A few months later, the engineering department moved to Swanley in Kent where the manufacturing division was based. Instead of just walking round a few corners to the old office, I now had to catch the 52 bus to Victoria and then take the train to Swanley. At Beckenham Junction station I was joined by Mr. Weber, who lived in Beckenham which gave me a chance to talk about other subjects than work and helped to create a more personal relationship with the "boss". Because my wages were only just enough to cover my living costs, the company paid my travel expenses. Every now and then I had to go through the production shop and take some measurement or other on one of the toilet roll machines which were all operated by young women or girls. Every time I came through the door they whistled. While I felt slightly flattered, it also made me feel contemptuous. I was far more interested in one of the attractive girls in the main office. Like most of the employees, she lived locally, so there was no way I could ask her out. However one day she told me that she sometimes came up to London at the weekend, which I took as a hint to meet. When I rashly suggested this, she immediately said that she would be free the next Saturday evening. We agreed to meet at the entrance of Kensington High Street underground station at 7.30 pm. I had no idea how this evening would be spent. I could not possibly take her home to my digs, and could just about afford two tickets to a cinema, so I decided to rely on her to come up with some bright ideas. At 7.30 I was at the station and waited and waited until it was 7.45. I then decided that she probably had changed her mind, and secretly believing that providence had saved me from a potentially embarrassing encounter, went home. The following Monday I went into the main office at lunchtime and was about to complain for being stood up, but before I could open my mouth she called me some pretty nasty names for not waiting longer. Apparently the train was held up getting into Victoria Station but she managed, she said, to get to Kensington by 7.50. However, the damage was done, The friendship was over.

Several times a week I visited a Jewish youth club near my digs, where one could learn to dance, play table tennis, attend lectures and socials and above all, meet girls. As I could't dance, I found the social evenings the most promising way to make contact with the opposite sex. The first time I attended such an evening we played musical chairs and I found myself competing with a particularly attractive girl for the remaining empty chair. Not being a gentleman, I pushed forward and sat down. To my amazement and delight, she promptly sat down on my lap.

As soon as the music started again, we both got up and without saying a word, I took her hand and wandered to the coffee counter. There over a coffee, we exchanged names and addresses. Her name was Jackie and it turned out that the house where she lived with her widowed mother was only about half a mile from my place. After chatting for a while I asked her whether I could walk her home and she said she'd be glad of the company. By the time we left the club at 10 o'clock, it was almost dark. I placed my arm round her waist and felt her pressing closer. This, I was sure, was going to be my real girl friend. It was not long before we arrived at her house, which was in a row of Victorian terrace houses with half a dozen steps leading to the unlit recessed front door.

In the street in front of the houses was a row of brick air raid shelters with concrete roofs, which were erected all over London during the war. There, in the dark recess of her door I plucked up the courage to kiss her. She stood still for moment, then withdrew her face and asked:

"Haven't you ever kissed a girl before"?

"'Course I have"

"Properly, I mean"

"Sure, what do you mean"?

"I'll show you" she said and planted her open lips on mine, forcing my lips apart.

We stood there for a while in a tight hug until she said:

"Let's go down into the shelter"

"What for?" I asked

"You know, do things we shouldn't be doing"

I then did one of the stupidest things of my life. I said that I respected her and proceeded to give her a lecture on the sad decline in morality, the danger of an unwanted pregnancy and the disgrace of being an unmarried mother etc. etc. She took a step back and looked at me in amazement.

"You're really sweet" she said.

"When can I take you to see a picture or something" I asked

"I'm free next Saturday evening"

"Right, I'll pick you up at seven"

We kissed again, properly this time, and I almost skipped my way home. I really liked her.

The next day I felt sick and was told by the chief draughtsman to go home and go to bed. As I only had her address, I immediately wrote her a letter as soon as I got home, explaining my predicament, hoping against hope that the Post Office would deliver it the next morning. All through the weekend I stayed in bed and thought about Jackie. I dreamt of holding her, kissing her and perhaps exploring her body, short of the real thing. Mrs Keane and a friend of hers plied me with orange juice and brandy, so that I was able to go back to work on Monday. On Tuesday evening, I heard the flap of the letter box and found an envelope addressed to me. I tore the envelope open and read:

"Dear Albert, It was lovely seeing you last week. I think you are an upright and decent young man and I respect you for it. However, it was just as well that you couldn't make our date, because I don't think it would be a good idea if we saw each other again. Yours, Jackie."

There it was. Just like that. No reason, no explanation. I was deeply depressed and wondered what I did wrong. Then the penny dropped and I realised what I said to her and what an absolute fool I was spouting all this morality stuff. From now on things will be different. I decided to go to the chemist in Westbourne Grove1 and a buy a packet of Durex, but when the girl behind the counter asked me what I wanted, I chickened out and settled for a tube of toothpaste.

There was of-course the possibility of explaining my behaviour when or if I met her again, but she never turned up at the club again and I certainly was not going to go to her house. Mrs. Keane was very sympathetic and tried to console me by assuring me several times that there were plenty more fish in the sea.

After several months of attending the dancing lessons at the club, I had enough confidence to actually ask a girl to take the floor with me. This opened up a new world, but although I walked many a girl home and kissed her good night, it was all pretty innocent. In the spring of 1946, I joined the Wingate Club, which catered for young people interested in the creation of a Jewish State . There I met my next real heartthrob, Edith. This relationship was really developing nicely, when at the beginning of May I received a letter from Bloomsbury House to get my papers together for an early departure to Southern Rhodesia. Having no passport, I had to go to the Passport Office to collect my travel permit and to Rhodesia House to pick up my Visa. There they also advised me to get myself immunised at the Welcome Institute in the Euston Road against Yellow Fever and other tropical diseases.

On the 7th June 1946, the day before the official V day, I received an express letter and telegram from Rhodesia House in London, informing me that a priority sea passage had been booked in a week's time to take me to South Africa and on to my parents in Bulawayo.

Passage to Africa

This gave me just a week to travel to Buckinghamshire to say good-bye to the Brutons, Emil, Auntie Maud and some of the other people in High Wycombe who had shown me great kindness during my time there. I also had to go to an office in Whitehall to enrol in the British Army and swear an oath of allegiance to King and Country, although I was still technically an enemy alien. The reason for this charade was that I was booked on a troop ship repatriating soldiers and airmen back to their homes in East and South Africa and I had to agree to place myself under the jurisdiction of the commanding officer.

UNION-CASTLE LINE.   R.M.S.   "ARUNDEL CASTLE."   19,118 TONS.

The R.M.S .Arundel Castle (S.S. Altmark)

The ship, a two-funnelled passenger liner of the Union Castle Line, which had seen better days, was the "Arundel Castle". Its conversion to a troop carrier did not improve its facilities. In fact after a few days at sea conditions got so bad that someone suggested we change her name to "Altmark", the infamous prison ship of the German battlecruiser "Admiral Graf Spee", which caused havoc among merchant ships in the South Atlantic but was eventually cornered by three British cruisers at the Battle of the River Plate.

Apart from me, there were a number of other civilians on board and I made friends with two men who coincidentally were also going to Bulawayo. One was a fitter and turner called Cyril and the other a coal miner from Durham called Dan White who informed us that everybody called him Chalky.

The troops on board were commanded by a small tubby Colonel, who was a strict disciplinarian. Every morning we had to parade on deck "with headgear". It was difficult to comply with this order because none of us had army, or any other formal headgear. We attended the first parade with a variety of head coverings. Dan (Chalky) wore a cloth cap, Cyril covered his head with a large handkerchief with a knot on each corner and I tied a towel round my head like a turban. When the colonel came to inspect us and saw our attire, he was furious. He went red in the face, stamped his feet, said something to the sergeant who accompanied him and stormed off. However nothing happened. The next day we paraded with bare heads, but no one seemed to care. The colonel certainly did not honour us with an inspection and after another day we did not even bother to turn up.

Apart from just missing a floating mine, our journey through the Atlantic and Mediterranean was uneventful. As the weather was warm and very sunny, I decided to get myself a bit of a tan, so that I would not show up as a raw immigrant in a country where, I assumed, everybody was a healthy brown. However, just one day on deck under the blue sky of the Mediterranean was enough to burn my legs to such an extent that I could hardly walk for two days. The army medical officer who treated me with lashings of Calamine lotion said I was lucky not to have been charged for "self inflicted wounds".

Sailing through the Suez Canal was uneventful but at Suez we picked up hundreds of East African Askaris who were being repatriated to Kenya. They were kept apart from the other passengers and service people and accommodated two decks below us. Four days later we anchored outside Aden and some of the service personnel were allowed to go on shore in the ship's boats, having been told over the Tannoy that the ship would sail at 6pm. Punctually at 6 o'clock the gangway on the side of the ship was raised ready to get under way, when we heard cries of "Stop, Stop" from two native motor boats ferrying half a dozen airmen and two WAFFs back from the port. However the gangway was not lowered and the two boats circled the ship in a desperate attempt to find another means of access. After about five minutes of pleas from the people in the boats to help to get them on board, someone cut the retaining ties of two emergency rope ladders, coiled up below the ship's railings. The rope ladders unfurled and were each quickly grabbed by one of the men. When he was a feet up the ladder, the climber was followed by one of the girls. All had clearly been indulging in some pretty heavy drinking, because half way up the ladder the girl passed out and fell back into the water. Immediately one chap dived into the sea from the deck to help her. Then the airman on the other ladder lost his grip and also fell into the sea. By that time a crowd had gathered on the railing and was shouting for the gangway to be lowered, while at the same time throwing some lifejackets and nearly all the lifebuoys on that side of the ship overboard. Tempers rose as friends of the people in the water threatened to lynch the colonel if he didn't lower the gangway. Ten minutes later, with the water around the ship full of buoys and empty life jackets and the floundering men and women each clutching one of the lifebuoys, the gangway rattled down and the wet and bedraggled miscreants clambered on board to be immediately arrested and put on a charge.

When we entered the Indian Ocean, the winds began to blow. The ship, which clearly had no stabilisers, rolled and bucked, making it impossible to walk without clutching a rail or rope. For two days I hardly ate because to reach our mess deck we had to pass through the quarters of the Askaris, none of whom appears to have been a sailor. There was vomit over their entire deck, so I just turned back and raced for the first open deck to get some fresh air. It was not until we reached Mombasa that I had a proper meal.

At Mombasa, history almost repeated itself. Just as we were pulling away from the quayside, 2 soldiers and 6 civilians arrived in a taxi and called after us to stop. Unlike the procedure at Aden, the ship did stop about half a mile from the quay. The people left behind then climbed down a steel ladder fixed to the concrete wall of the quay, to reach a floating caisson in the form of an egg-grate of six compartments. One of the civilians slipped while on the ladder and fell head first through one of the holes of the caisson. while his head and shoulders went through the hole into the water, his hips got stuck. The other men pulled him out of the water and all of them climbed into a native motor boat, which had miraculously appeared as if ordered. They then raced out to the ship where they were helped on board at a door on the side of the hull, a few feet above the water. We later learnt that the man had a broken pelvis and was taken straight to hospital when we reached Durban. Not a good homecoming!

On 6 July 1946 we berthed in Durban and were greeted on the dock by the singing lady, who I learnt later, welcomed every troopship which entered Durban with a song, amplified by a huge megaphone, since the beginning of the war. The next day, Cyril, Dan and I boarded the train to Johannesburg, where I was met by relatives of my mother who gave me supper, showed me around Johannesburg and plied me with sweets and fruit, some of which I hadn't seen for six years. Later that evening, we changed trains and set off to our final destination Bulawayo, Southern Rhodesia, where we arrived two days later.

Rhodesia (now Zimbabwe)

My mother and father met me at the station. After seven years of separation, I was surprised how little they had changed. The perfect weather, the bright sun and clean air was in sharp contrast to the rainy atmosphere in Southampton four weeks earlier. I immediately fell in love with the place. As we drove back my parents took me on a tour through the centre of Bulawayo which was far more modern than I expected. I was particularly impressed by the wide streets in the centre of town which were in effect dual carriageways and the prestigious town hall surrounded by beautiful well kept gardens.

Bulawayo Town Hall

When we arrived at my parent's house we were met by their houseboy.

"This is Samson" my mother said.

"Hello, Samson" I said, "glad to meet you" and shook his hand. He beamed with amazement.

My mother drew me aside and whispered: "You don't shake hands with the boys here"

Oh dear, my first encounter with Rhodesian apartheid.

Within hours, my uncle, aunt and cousins and numerous friends arrived to welcome me.

This, I decided will be my home for ever and ever. To add to my joy, my parents had bought me a wonderful coming home present. A shining new Raleigh bike with racing style handlebars and pedal straps.

One of my first objectives was to find a job. During one of the many stays with Auntie Maud in Gerrards Cross, I had met a young German Engineer, Max Brauer, who was married to a friend of Aunty Maud's daughter Betty. When I told him that I had ambitions to become an engineer, he argued strongly that the best way to get a good practical understanding of what engineering is all about was to take up an apprenticeship and study the theoretical aspects at the same time in the evenings or in day release courses.

As my parents were not in a position to finance my attendance at a University in South Africa and since I was in effect stateless, there was no opportunity to receive any grants or scholarships for full-time study. I therefore had no choice but to take Max Brauer's advice and find a firm who would take me on as an engineering apprentice at the relatively old age of 19.

Parallel with my practical training it was essential that I continued with my theoretical studies which could be pursued at the Bulawayo Technical College up to South African Engineering Diploma standard. I was fortunate in having a very enthusiastic maths teacher in a Mr. Owen, who offered

My parents and a friend at their house in Bulawayo

to give me extra lessons at his home on a Sunday morning. He absolutely refused any payment, calling the extra tuition a labour of love. One of the more interesting topics was differential calculus and I was so intrigued by maxima/minima that I wanted to find a practical application. Every evening I had a cup of cocoa. The Bournville cocoa tin was quite tall and I always had difficulty in extracting the last spoonful when the tin was close to empty. It suddenly occurred to me that perhaps here was the opportunity to apply my newly acquired knowledge, so I measured the area of the tin plate (including the lid) and worked out the volume. Then I applied maxima/minima and discovered that if the height of the tin is the same as its diameter, the area of plate could be reduced by about 12% while the volume remained the same. I then wrote a letter to Cadbury/Bournville explaining my findings and enclosing my calculations. Three weeks later I received their answer thanking me for my interest in their products and the calculations which they had not checked but were sure were correct. However, they explained that the existing tin had greater "eyeabilty" on the shelves and the cost of changing their machinery would be prohibitive. A few days later I received the most enormous three layer box of chocolates I had ever seen. Now I had the chance to show my gratitude to Mr Owen. The following Sunday morning I presented the chocolates to his wife.

With the help of friends of my parents, I was introduced to the directors of every, by Rhodesian standards, major engineering company, but although they appeared to be impressed by my scholastic achievements, they had either no vacancies or thought I should have applied when I was younger.

At the time my father worked for a firm making furniture and, in order to keep me busy until something suitable presented itself, he arranged for me to get a taste of some industrial experience in their production shops. For the next three months I learnt how to use a planer, a dovetail machine, a power saw, a sander and a host of other woodworking machines, but my heart was not in it. I even turned down an offer by the managing director of the firm to study furniture design in South Africa at the company's expense.

Engineering Training

Then came the breakthrough. A new company had just been established out on what was called, "the heavy industrial estate" to produce metal products for the building industry. Appropriately it was called Rhodesian Metal Products (RMP) and they were happy to take me on as their first apprentice. Entering into an apprenticeship I discovered was quite a formal procedure. The "Form of Contract of Apprenticeship" had to be issued by the Chief Industrial Inspector and signed by a magistrate. I also agreed to join the Amalgamated Engineering Union (AEU). The document set out my rates of pay for the next five years from 7 pence per hour to 2 shillings and three pence per hour and all the other terms and conditions. Unlike the practice in England, where the first year apprentice was often treated as a dogs body fetching the foreman's cigarettes, in Rhodesia I was allocated my own Boy, in my case a young African labourer who cleaned my machines, handed me my tools, washed my white overalls over the weekend and, after an unusually cold night, even arrived half an hour before me to warm up the handles of my lathe with a blow-lamp. I was fortunate to be in a new company where from day one, the skilled journeymen were happy to teach me how to operate a lathe, shaper, grinder, milling machine and drill press, as well as teaching me electric arc welding and the proper use of hand tools.

Soon the company decided to build their own mechanised foundry, the first in Rhodesia, and I helped to erect the furnace and the row of air operated moulding machines called jolters because after pouring the sand into the moulding boxes located on the machine, the main body jolted rapidly up and down. When the installation was complete, all the directors and other VIPs were invited to a grand opening to witness the first batch of castings coming off the production line. I was allocated to keep an eye on one of the white unskilled operators of one of the jolters. After removing the finished mould box, the body of the machine was lowered straight onto my right foot, which I inadvertently and stupidly, had placed under it. In agony I screamed: "Lift it off". But instead of pulling the lift lever, the operator pulled the jolt lever, and the body of the machine hammered down on my toe at a rate of four blows a second. By the time I managed to extract it the nail of my big toe had just about come off and I ended up in the office with the wife of the managing director bandaging me up. My escapade halted the demonstration run and the great celebration fizzled out. I was off work for three days and fully expected the sack when I returned, but everyone was very sympathetic and, a little unfairly, blamed the operator for pulling the wrong lever.

RMP produced a large number of products ranging from brass padlocks, drain fittings in brass, aluminium or cast iron to trailers and wheelbarrows. Perhaps the range was too wide or the demand was overestimated, because after eighteen months they went out of business. The Industrial Council then arranged for me to be transferred to a well established engineering company called O. Connolly & Co, where I finished my apprenticeship. I addition to gaining further experience in working on various new machine tools such as capstan lathes and bore-mills, I also had the opportunity of working in the foundry, making the sand moulds for castings which I later machined. Because of my good examination results, my official apprenticeship was reduced from 4 years to 3 years and I was paid the full wages of a journeyman for the last year, six months of which were spent in the drawing office. My days in the workshops were over.

At the end of my apprenticeship, I left Connolly's and joined a local structural engineering company as a draughtsman. This exposed me to a new branch of engineering which had always attracted me. This was the world of towers, cranes, buildings and bridges, the big brothers of the things I tried to build with my Meccano set. The machines we designed and built at Conolly's were mainly for the mining industry and followed well proven, tried and tested designs unchanged for the last ten years. There was little scope or need for designing from first principles. With structural engineering however, things were different. Every building or structure had to be designed from scratch to resist the imposed forces which were different for every construction. At last I could apply the formulae and principles I had learnt for my Theory of Structures examination. Now I had the opportunity to learn how to design, draw and detail both steelwork and reinforced concrete structures under the supervision of a highly qualified structural engineer who later became the local partner of one of the biggest firms of Consulting Engineers in the UK.

In 1947 My parents persuaded my sister Hella, who trained as a pharmacist in London to join us in Bulawayo. After nine years the whole family was together again. Hella soon found a job in one of the local pharmacies, but after 11 months she felt that the life in Bulawayo was too restrictive and she returned to England to obtain the required Royal Pharmaceutical Society qualifications. In 1953 she got a grant to study at the Chelsea School of Pharmacy where she obtained her Phc and in 1957 she joined the British Weleda where after only 10 years became the company's Technical Director and Joint Managing Director. This was of direct benefit to me, as when I noticed I was loosing my hair, she advised me to use Weleda Hair Lotion, which completely stopped the fall-out. She then kept me supplied with this lotion until her retirement.

Zionism

The Jewish community in Bulawayo boasted a magnificent building called the Guild Hall which served as a venue for meetings, wedding receptions, concerts, and even indoor sports events. It was not long after my arrival that I was invited by the son of one of our neighbours to one of the Zionist Youth meetings which took place monthly at the Guild Hall. I had had a brush with a Zionist youth organisation at the Wingate Club in England but felt that the establishment of a separate Jewish state went against the then euphoric belief in international integration, not separation. I argued that another country meant another frontier, which meant another potential war. Surely after such a terrible war the world, and specifically the United Nations Organisation, would ban persecution of all minorities and, by the simple process of full integration would eliminate separatism and bigotry.

However, at the first Zionist Youth meeting I attended at the Guild Hall, my rather naive view of the new world order was shattered, when the speaker justified the need for a Jewish State by simply pointing out that even in a new country like Southern Rhodesia, Jews, however well established, were still regarded as not being quite acceptable. I was shocked to learn that Jewish business men and professionals were not accepted as members of the "Bulawayo Club", which resulted in the Jewish community building their own club a few miles out of town. The only way we can regain our self-respect is to become "normalised" the speaker argued, "have our own country, our

On my BSA 250 cc Motorbike

own industry, farmers, builders, engineers, doctors, universities, and even our own policemen. Only then will we have the same status in the world as the people of other countries, who have their own homeland with their own embassies to protect them when abroad". The argument made sense, and I joined the Zionist Youth Organisation.

Over the next few years I became what was known as an armchair Zionist, defined as a Jew who persuades another Jew to collect money from another Jew to send another Jew to Israel. I rose in the ranks to become chairman of the Bulawayo Zionist Youth Organisation and became a member of the South African Youth Council.

Then on the 29 November 2047 the United Nations, at a meeting at which America and the Soviet Union actually voted on the same side, agreed to the establishment of a Jewish homeland in Palestine. All our dreams had come true. The Jews were no longer just the "wandering tribe" of shopkeepers and money lenders. Israel would become a model for the rest of the world to follow. In a sense I also saw it as a "mission accomplished" and my interest in active participation of Zionist activities waned. However, most importantly, it engendered in me a renewed self-confidence and self-respect which I had never experienced before. At last the feeling of inferiority engraved into my subconscious by the constant abusive ranting of the Nazis was gone. The air was fresher and the light brighter.

Motor Bike and first car

Bulawayo at this time was not blessed with a public transport system, so the only way one could get into town or to one's place of work was to go by bike or car. As I lived at home, I could start saving enough money to buy a second hand BSA motorbike which gave me a whole new degree of freedom.

There was nothing more exhilarating than to ride out into the open country dressed only in a shirt over my kidney belt and a pair of shorts and sandals, open the throttle to 60 mph and feel the wind through my hair. My mother on the other hand, was not so enthusiastic and was ever fearful that one day I would come off and end up in hospital.

One night as I was returning home from an evening class I saw a group of people crossing the road from left to right towards the central parking strip in Bulawayo's wide two lane Main Street. Instinctively, I slowed down swerved to the left to make sure I missed them, when one of them ran back and straight into my front wheel. I flew over the handlebars and landed on my head, smashing my goggles into my right eye. When I came to, I was in a cafe being bandaged up by the owner and some customers. The man I hit, or rather who hit me, was lying motionless on the pavement also being administered to by bystanders. A few minutes later in the ambulance, he regained consciousness. We were each lying in bunks separated by a walkway and the first thing we did was to reach across the aisle and shake hands, grateful perhaps that we were both still alive.

When I came out of hospital a day later, my parents left me in no doubt that the motorbike had to go. I borrowed some money from my uncle and bought an ancient 1932 Hillman Minx which had the advantage that I could

The 1932 Hillman Minx

date girls without having to ask my father for his car. In fact, it was on the back seat of this car that I lost my virginity.

For its age, the car ran beautifully and I had no cause to even open the bonnet. Then one day I noticed that the floor-mounted gear lever seemed a bit closer to my left leg than usual. The next day, as I got in to go to work, I found that when I put it into first gear, the lever touched my left knee. This time I decided to open the bonnet and found that one of the engine supports had cracked and broken away leaving the engine leaning at 30 degrees from the vertical. However, as was still firing as normal, I simply drove straight into our welding shop at work where the engine was jacked into the vertical again and the broken bracket welded together. Over the next year more and more parts of the car needed replacing or repairing, which meant that I learnt great deal about engines and other components, which stood me in good stead for the future.

Samson

One day I noticed that my exhaust pipe emitted a lot more smoke than usual. It did not require a knowledge of rocket science to realise that the car needed either new piston rings or a complete re-bore. This entailed removing the cylinder head and lying on your back under the car to remove the sump and the connecting rods, a tedious, lengthy and very uncomfortable operation. I could foresee having to get underneath the car for one reason or another in the future, so I decided to dig a 5 feet deep maintenance pit in the driveway to the garage, to enable me to at least work under the car while standing upright. I could not have done the work without the help of our houseboy Samson who actually volunteered to do most of the digging, while I built the brick walls to keep the sides from collapsing.

A week after the pit was finished, Samson, who was with my parents from the day they first set up their own home in Rhodesia, announced that in two days time he would be returning to his village for two or three weeks. The next day he presented his temporary replacement, Jeremiah, to my mother assuring her that he was "very good", but it was left unclear whether that referred to his character or work ethic.

The new boy started work on the day Samson left, but on the following Saturday he did not return from his nightly visit to the "Location", the only area of Bulawayo where the Africans could have their own shops, dance halls, and drinking establishments etc.

Just before noon that day an African policeman immaculate in this smart starched khaki uniform with creases on his shorts so sharp that one could almost cut one's fingers on them, rang our door bell. My mother and I opened the door together.

"Good morning Madam, do you have a boy called Jeremiah?" he asked in impeccable English

"Yes, but he is not here" answered my mother

"Well, he won't be returning to you Madam, because he is in jail"

"Why, what has he done?"

"He was playing cards in the Location and split another boy's head with an axe"

"What?" my mother gasped

"Sorry to bring you such bad news Madam, Good bye Madam" and with that he left.

"How are we going to find a replacement until Samson comes back?" I asked

"We'll just have to manage without him for a while" she said.

The next day, again just before noon, there was a knock on the kitchen door.

I opened the door. There stood Samson.

"Sorry about Jeremiah, Baas, the Missus will need me" was all he said and came into the kitchen.

"How on earth did he find out what happened ?" I asked my father

"Bush telegraph" he answered.

We never did discover how he found out so quickly about Jeremiah. I was deeply touched by his loyalty and concern for my mother for whom and with whom he had worked for over 30 years until the day he had a drink too many and was run over and killed by a car in the Location.

I was advised by the hospital to see a specialist about my right eye with which I could only see objects a few yards away. The only eye consultant in Bulawayo, Dr. Shankman, examined me and told me bluntly that I would never see properly with that eye again. Apparently I had mild concussion which produced a blood clot over the "yellow spot" on the retina. This is the spot where one focuses on objects a long way off, i.e. infinity. I then sent Dr. Shankman's report to another eye specialist in Johannesburg, who replied that if Dr. Shankman's diagnosis was correct, there is nothing more that he could do for me. I therefore resigned myself to the fact that I would have to learn to live with one eye, but my dear mother would not give up. She learnt that there was a new doctor, called Dr. Greenwood, just arrived from England who happened to be the honorary surgeon of the Bulawayo Motor Cycle Club, and who had cured a rash around my

Samson

cousin's eye. Although I tried to convince her that such a visit would be a waste of time and money as a rash around the eye is a very different kettle of fish to a damaged retina, I eventually agreed to see him just to placate her. After Dr. Greenwood examined me he simply said "Hm, I think we can cure this", and prescribed a course of eye drops to be administered daily for four weeks. These drops apparently dissolved the blood clot, and at my last visit I cold read the last line on the eye chart. This convinced me that in future one should always ask for a second or third opinion.

Messing around with my ancient Hillman was actually quite fun, especially as some of my friends were keen to help me. I subscribed to two motoring magazines and was particularly taken by an advertisement of the post-war MG TC. This was the car for me.

Obviously I did not have enough money for a new one, but my father knew a dealer who had just taken delivery of one under a year old and could let me have it at a reasonable price. If ever there was a car which made friends it is an MG. Everyone wanted to ride in this red shiny sports car, especially girls. Even Rover, our Alsatian, would jump into the open car in the hope of being taken for a drive. He would sit upright on the passenger seat and stick his head above the windscreen to catch the wind, but because of the cut-out doors, every time I came to a right hand bend in the road Ihad to grab his collar to stop him being flung right out of the car.

The MG Club

Shortly after getting the car I joined the newly formed MG Club which had twenty members, nineteen of which drove an MG of one type or another. We had regular rallies, hill climbs, hill descents, gymkhanas and races. At one race, on the narrow track owned by the Bulawayo Motor Cycle Club, I was neck on neck with another MG TC, and as we approached a sharp left hand bend, I knew that the last one to brake would go into the lead. I must have held back just a little too long for the bend came up quicker than I thought and I slammed on the brakes and at the same time double de-clutched and pushed the gear lever from 3rd into 1st gear. The rev counter swung round the dial, the engine roared, and as the car slowed down just in time to enable me to go round the bend, a pall of black smoke billowed out of the exhaust pipe. I had blown every piston ring including the oil rings. As I pulled out of the bend there was just enough power to enable me to complete the circuit and limp back into the pits.

Rover in the driving seat of the MG

I had two friends who usually acted as co-driver on the rallies. One was another German emigrant who had served an engineering apprenticeship in Rhodesia called was Ernest Lewin and the other was Jurick Goldwasser, a very talented electronics engineer, who was the nephew of the American Senator Goldwater. (He later became interested in local politics and was elected mayor of Bulawayo).

Although I took part in all the events organised by he MG Club, I only ever won once. The occasion was a timed hill climb in the rainy season, which included crossing a dam wall the top of which was submerged in about a foot of water, well above the height of the exhaust pipe. I was the last car to make the run with my friend Jurick as co-driver. The approach to the top of the dam was a very steep ramp which had to be negotiated very slowly before entering the water. As I approached the ramp I applied the brakes, but because they were wet from going through a number of deep puddles, they failed to stop the car. As a result we hit the water with an enormous splash, the cockpit floor was flooded and Jurick shouted "Get her into 1st and keep the revs up". I followed his instructions and we roared across the wall forcing the water out of the exhaust. On the other side was the hill we had to

A typical timed speed event

climb and I was surprised to learn that we had the fastest time for the simple reason that we could not slow down before we hit the water.

Soon car enthusiasts driving other makes wanted to join the club and the name was changed to the Bulawayo Motoring Club (BMC). We continued to have rallies, but no more races or rough stuff like timed hill descents and I lost interest.

Every motoring club has at least one dare-devil driver and ours was Matt Dugdale, often referred to as Mad Matt. During the war he was in the Commandos and was captured when the Germans invaded Crete. With the aid of a German girl who suppled the civilian clothes, he escaped, but was soon recaptured and although brutally interrogated, he did not divulge the girl's name. After the war, when life for many people in Germany was desperate, he managed to make contact with the girl and re-payed her by persuading the Government to issue a visa for her and her parents to settle in Rhodesia, where her father opened a factory for making clay bricks and tiles.

Matt and his wife would win quite a few events in his MG TC, mainly because he loved taking risks. On of the most dangerous sections of an event cooked up by the organising committee was a timed hill descent on a very steep farm track covered with large stones and deep ruts which ran right across the road. When my turn came I started to accelerate down the hill but soon found that the terrain was pretty dangerous. The car was being thrown around as I hit one rut after another and my co-driver was crouched low in the cockpit clinging onto the grab handle on the dashboard for dear life. I breathed a sigh of relief when we reached the bottom of the hill with all my wheels intact, only to be told by the marshal that he forgot to press his stop watch.

Matt at a race meeting

"You'll have to go down again" he said

"You've got to be joking," I replied, "this course is a bloody death trap"

The next car to make the descent was Matt with his wife as co-driver. As usual he went just that little bit faster than the others. When he was about half way down the hill, he hit a rut with such force that the spokes of one of his front wheels buckled and the car rolled over on its side. Matt and his wife were thrown out and landed on the stone strewn track, badly lacerated on their arms and legs. That section of the event was stopped, and the injured couple were taken to hospital in the only four seater MG roadster taking part.

As the car rolled over, all the four wheels collapsed and the folded down windscreen smashed. However, the four wheels were replaced by the spare wheels taken from four other MG TCs and the car actually continued to participate fully in the rest of the event with another driver.

As well as driving an MG, Matt also owned one of the new Triumph 500cc Tiger motor bikes which he raced at meetings organised by the Bulawayo Motorcycle Club. Because he knew that I liked engines, he asked me to become his pit mechanic whenever there was a local race. However his attitude was that speed was more important than safety.

On one occasion I found that one of the footrests had cracked and asked him not to take part in the race.

"Will a cracked footrest slow me down?" he asked.

"No, but if it falls off you may not be able to finish", I replied

He decided to ride in the race and I decided to quit as his mechanic.

Matt's crashed MG after new wheels had been fitted.

A month later he took part in a race in Salisbury (now Harare) and hit a pot hole in the track. The telescopic forks seized up and Matt with his bike somersaulted onto the course. As he landed, the saddle hit him in the back of the neck just below his crash helmet and killed him.

At about that time I was dating a very attractive girl who was a fashion designer and part time model called Betsy. She accompanied me on some of the longer MG Club rallies which involved overnight stays in the bush under a clear moonlit sky. We made a kind of lager by parking the cars in a circle with a camp fire in the centre. Naturally we all had separate sleeping bags except one man, Frank, an ex policeman who brought a sleeping bag large enough to accommodate him and his girl friend Lucy. As the camp fire died and it was time to turn in, everyone watched in amazement as this girl just stripped to her panties and climbed into the sleeping bag. As Frank unbuckled his belt, he must have become aware of everyone watching him and wondering whether he would join his girlfriend, so he just said:

"It'll get too bloody cold to sleep in the open" and climbed into the sack.

At a typical rally

Eventually Betsy and I drifted apart and a few months later she married an American mining engineer who literally had the Midas touch. A year earlier he had bought an old gold mine to recover and process the waste from the spoil heap which usually contained rare metals. One day he went underground and chipped away at the end of an old adit and uncovered a gold seam which made him a millionaire.

At the grand wedding reception I congratulated her father, with whom I had always got on very well, and as we shook hands he said: "Albert, it should have been you".

The girl friend that followed Betsy was Jane. She was introduced to me by my MG Club friend Matt Dugdale. At weekends we would drive out into the Matopos hills where Cecil Rhodes was buried, and lie in the shade of one of the great stone boulders away from the tourist area where no one could see what we were up to. Because in Rhodesia there is no drawn out dusk as in Europe, we normally stayed until the sun just reached the horizon to make sure we reached the main road before it got dark. On one occasion we had just reached the track to Rhodes' grave about half a mile from the main road,

Betsy

when the engine spluttered and died. No petrol. The MG, instead of having a petrol gauge on the dashboard, it had a green warning light which lit up when there was only a gallon left in the tank. Unfortunately, the terminals of the float mechanism in the tank were slightly corroded and the warning lamp did not light up.

Here we were, stuck in the bush in an open car in wildlife country and getting dark. By sheer good fortune the last visitor to Rhodes' grave must have left after us and as the headlights of the car came towards us, we both ran into the road and frantically waved our arms to slow him down. The vehicle which stopped was a Chevrolet pick-up truck. We explained our predicament and after asking the couple in the truck to give us a lift to the Matopos hotel we clambered into the back, thanking fate for delivering us from a potentially serious situation. At the hotel I telephoned my father to drive to the Matopos Hotel with a can of petrol and a funnel. He was not at all pleased at the prospect of driving the 35 miles to the hotel in the dark, but I am sure my mother gave him no choice.

Rhodes' grave at Matopos

An hour later he arrived in a terrible mood, grumbling about my carelessness etc. etc. and we drove back to the abandoned MG, emptied the can of petrol into the tank and headed for home. Jane was not impressed by this episode. The real possibility of spending the night in a car with only a canvas roof and un-lockable doors in the wilds of the Matopos only sunk in on the way back. She hardly spoke and only answered in monosyllables and I knew that I was definitely out of favour.

I decided to let things cool down for a few days and a week later rang her to make another date. The call was answered by a girlfriend who stayed with her, who advised me that it might be better if I did not contact her again. This only spurred me on to drive out to her house to confront her, only to find another car parked outside. In a mixture of dismay and anger, I knocked on the door which was opened by a man called Nat whom I knew from the BMC but never liked. Words were exchanged, insults were thrown and we ended up in the road throwing punches. By chance I landed a blow on his nose and he fell back bleeding profusely. By that time Jane came running out of the house, saw her new friend kneeling on the road with his face covered in blood. She put her arms round his shoulders, called me a bully and a savage and told me she never wanted to see me again. I won the fight but lost the girl. Never, I promised myself, would I ever physically fight over a woman again.

I drove home miserable and dejected. I suddenly realised I needed to get away and be by myself for a few days. The next day I asked the firm for a few days leave which was due to me, packed a small suitcase with my toilet bag, a clean bush shirt, shorts and socks and drove off after an early breakfast to Inyanga and the Vumba mountains in eastern Rhodesia. This area, known as the Switzerland of the South, has probably the most beautiful and unspoilt landscape of Rhodesia with high waterfalls, rugged mountains and masses of wild life including elephant. That evening and 370 miles later I booked in at the Leopard Rock Hotel and breathed in the pure mountain air. The hotel was almost deserted and I went to bed as soon as I had had my dinner. The next morning I got up early so that I could visit the Pungwe Falls and Troutbeck Inn where one could choose the trout one wanted for lunch from a shallow trough by the hotel. There was one other guest having breakfast, an attractive brunette wearing a khaki bush shirt and shorts. She looked up as I entered the dining room and gave me a faint smile.

"Good morning, lovely day" I said, as I sat down a couple of tables away

"Isn't it just" was the reply. End of conversation.

I finished my breakfast before her and sauntered over to her table.

"What brings you to this part of the world" I started

"I just felt I had to get away for a bit"

"Snap" I said

I pulled up a chair on the opposite side of the table and said:

"Man problem"?

She smiled: "Sort of"

"Keep away from them, they're bad news"

She gave a short laugh "You should know"

I then proceeded to tell her that I too had to find a change of scenery and soon we were exchanging the reasons for our trip. I asked her to come with me to Pungwe, but she had already made plans to explore Inyanga. So we agreed to meet for dinner that evening when we came back to the hotel. It turned out she was a nurse from Johannesburg and for the next two days we lay on deckchairs on the hotel terrace, talked about everything under the sun and discussed our predicaments in the knowledge that after we parted we would never meet again. She then drove back home and I went on to Umtali (now Mutare) where I knew that Matt Dugdale was taking part in a BMC car rally. I drove into the car park near the pits when my heart missed a beat. There, in Nat's open car sat Jane. I quickly reversed the car out of the car park and drove straight back to Bulawayo.

Jurick in his sleeping bag   *With Jurick on a prospecting trip*

At that time the world was rearming and two minerals common in Rhodesia were suddenly in great demand. Asbestos and Scheelite, one of the ores of tungsten. Many adventurous people spent their spare time prospecting for these desirable minerals and some, including Betsy's husband, made a fortune. Jurick and I decided that we both deserved to be rich and try our luck at prospecting at week-ends. Armed with prospecting hammers an ultra-violet lamp and two large thermos flasks of cold water, we set of in his Austin 10 tramping over over the bush in areas which were rumoured to have deposits. In Rhodesia any prospector was allowed to walk over any farm or ranch and dig a hole, provided it was not within 100 yards of a homestead or spoilt the crops. In fact we never got as far as digging, because we had a rule that when the water ran out we would turn back. On one occasion we asked a farmer whether we could cross his land and he proudly told us that he had already registered a stake for mining purposes over the whole area, but he offered to show us what he had already found. This was a long drift cut into a small hill, high enough to walk upright. As soon as we entered the dark cavern, he switched on his ultra-violet lamp and the nuggets of scheelite in the rock blinked back at us just like the gems in the dwarf's cave from Walt Disney's "Snow White and the Seven Dwarves". The man was sitting on a fortune and we left somewhat disheartened and very envious.

One weekend we decided to explore the area at the edge of the Wankie National Park. At night we slept under the stars in sleeping bags protected by

Albert Lester

two large mosquito nets hung from the car door handles. Next morning we were woken by girlish laughter and found ourselves surrounded by about a dozen young bare breasted African girls, pointing at us and giggling with delight. As we wanted to get up but were in our birthday suits, we tried to shoo them away with shouts of "hamba". That made them laugh even more, so Jurick simply picked up his 303 Lee Enfield rifle which we always had with us and placed the

The MG and the Piper Cub

butt on his shoulder. That had the desired effect for they fled shrieking and we could clamber out of the sleeping bags and get dressed.

After a few weeks of very amateurish and utterly unrewarding prospecting, we decided to ask our girl friends to come with us. This turned out to be the death of prospecting but the birth of some enjoyable weekends.

At about the time of my break-up with Jane, I learnt that a new young people's group was about to be opened in one of Bulawayo's community halls. Its aim was to meet weekly to discuss current issues, have debates and occasional dances and generally enable similarly minded people to mix socially. The group was run by a young social worker called Xandrien, who had just arrived from South Africa and what I took to be her boyfriend Alan, a slightly overweight insurance agent. Both Jurick and I were intrigued by the idea, especially the debating prospects and decided to go to the inaugural meeting. We were both impressed by the two speakers who explained the aims and objectives and with about twenty other attendees enrolled. It was not long before I realised what an extraordinary girl Xandrien was. She was not only very bright and energetic but was also very good looking, and when, over a cup of coffee after a debate to which I contributed, albeit only from from the floor, she informed me that Alan was only a good friend, I took the hint and asked her whether she would like to come prospecting with us. That was the beginning of a loving relationship which lasted until the day I returned to England.

One day she was visited by one of her well-heeled Afrikaans ex-boy-friends from Johannesburg, who arrived in his own Piper Cub aeroplane. He offered to take her for a spin in his plane, but she only agreed on condition that I came along too. Reluctantly the fellow agreed, but learning that I had never been in a light plane before, was clearly determined to make the flight as uncomfortable as possible for me.

He flew over the Matopos Hills, Rhodes' Grave and the Shangani Memorial, erected to commemorate the ill fated patrol of 34 of British South Africa Police troopers who were killed by the Matabele. When the plane was over the memorial, he cut the engined and side-slipped down. I realised that he was trying to frighten me, and although he succeeded, I could hardly show it in front of Xandrien. So in an attempt to display my non-concern, I took out my camera and began to photograph the memorial with a number of shots as we got closer and closer to the ground. Just when the image of the memorial almost filled my viewfinder and I really got worried, he restarted the motor, opened the throttle and zoomed up into the blue sky. Despite my

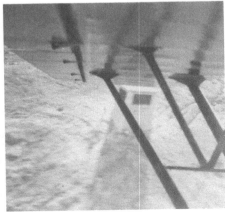

Shots of the Shangani Memorial

pretended heroism I must have gone pretty pale, because Xandrien asked him to take us back to the airport.

A few months later when I had to tell her that I had to return to England to finish my studies she burst into tears. We both promised to write to each other, but sadly time and distance can be very erosive and after a few exchanges she wrote to me that she would be returning to South Africa. Perhaps she went back to her flying Dutchman.

Theory and Practice

The highest qualification I could achieve in Rhodesia without actually going to university, was the South African Engineering Diploma, which was accepted on a subject for subject basis by the Institution of Mechanical Engineers for Associate Membership. One of the examinations for the Diploma was to design, draw and submit full calculations for one of three topics: A petrol engine, a horizontal three-throw pump or a Lancashire boiler. I chose the Lancashire boiler because I believed it to be the easiest option, although I knew that while this type of boiler was now way out of date, the fundamental principles of pressure vessel design and thermo-dynamics still applied. Little did I know that some twenty-five years later I would be a project director with Foster Wheeler, a company which built about a third of all the huge 500 MegaWatt utility power-station boilers in the UK. Frank on the other hand, the only other candidate from Bulawayo, chose the pump. We were given six months to submit our work and we both spent every Saturday morning at the Technical College working in the same room on our designs. On the last Saturday before the submission date we put the finishing touches to our drawings, which had to be in ink on drawing linen. Although we discussed some common problems during the six months, we were concentrating on our own designs, but now on the last day we were admiring each other's drawings. I watched my fellow candidate stencilling the title: HORIZONTAL THREE-THROW PUMP when I noticed that he had actually drawn a vertical pump.

"God almighty" he cried when I pointed it out, hitting his forehead with his palm.

"What have I done. This is a disaster"

We called the teacher who was our supervisor, who was equally horrified.

"Do you think I can get an extension for a re-draw"? asked Frank

"I doubt it, you'll just have to submit it as it is and enclose a letter of apology of some sort" replied the teacher, "but" he added, "if you like, I will also send a letter to the Examination Board explaining that the fundamental design principles are obviously the same, whether the pump is vertical or horizontal."

"If the principles are the same and the calculations are the same, why don't you just make a new drawing. It doesn't have to be as perfect as this one", I suggested.

"Its got to go on Monday" he moaned, "It took two months to draw this one, how can I re-draw this and trace it in one day"

He decided to follow the advice of the teacher.

Two months later we got the exam results. I passed, but Frank's design was rejected. I felt really bitter about his failure. Surely the examination was to test the knowledge and skill of the candidate, not whether the damn thing is standing up or lying down. It reminded me of the time I got zero marks for my book cover design at school. Bureaucracy, it appears, always wins.

After a year I suddenly had a call from Bob Ryan the chief engineer at Conolly's. He told me that he was setting up on his own and wondered whether I would join him. I did not really want to leave Hogarth, but Bob and I had got on extremely well while I was in the drawing office for the last year of my apprenticeship and I learnt a lot from him. More out of loyalty than anything else, I accepted his offer and certainly had the opportunity to design some interesting mechanisms. I did warn him though, that I would have to return to England to continue my studies, because the South African Engineering Diploma had to be augmented by additional Institution examinations if

I wanted to become an Associate Member of the Institution of Mechanical Engineers. (AMIMechE). Although I had not kept in touch with Mrs Keane with whom I had boarded when I was last in London, I wrote to her to inform her of my plan to return and asked whether I could renew the previous arrangement for a few weeks until I found my feet in London. She immediately wrote back to say that nothing would please her more. That removed a great worry from my mind, as I had not really thought out any realistic alternative.

Return to England

I decided that the best time to leave would be in the Autumn of 1952, in time for the start of the next academic year. I managed to get a berth on the Stirling Castle sailing from Cape Town and two days before I was due to leave, I received my call-up papers for the Rhodesian Territorial Army, having been naturalised as a British Subject a year earlier. However, because I was leaving to continue my studies, I was given a leave of absence until my return.

The prospect of leaving Rhodesia was not easy. I had grown to love the easygoing life style, the beautiful weather which was utterly predictable. You could plan a picnic between February and October in the guaranteed knowledge it would be a fine day. I loved the wide open spaces, the clean air and the freedom from petty regulations. I knew that my parents would be heartbroken at losing me again and I had grown really fond of Xandrien, but they all accepted the fact that there was no other way for me to get a degree and membership of one of the major Engineering Institutions.

I knew that I would never be able to buy a car in England, so I decided to take my MG with me. This meant driving it down to Cape Town and putting it in the hold of the Stirling Castle. To be able to enter South Africa one needed a Carnet issued by the AA. When I filled in the necessary documents the AA official asked me:

"Do you have a gun"?

"Yes, I have a 32 Browning Automatic" I replied

"Make sure you take it with you, and don't stop for anyone lying in the road" he advised

My mother cried openly and my father had tears in his eyes as I drove my open MG out of the yard of our house dressed only in shorts, a bush shirt and a zip up leather jacket which covered my gun belt with the bullets in loops, cowboy style, and the leather holster of the Browning. With the hood folded down and only a baseball cap to protect me from the sun, I drove off on my three-day journey through the Karoo desert to Cape Town.

About half way between Bulawayo and the border with South Africa I saw another MG coming towards me. As he passed me the driver waved and hooted. When I looked in my rear view mirror I noticed he had pulled up, so I stopped and reversed towards him. The driver got out of the car, smiled and said "Snap". We both had red MG TCs. He offered me a cigarette, we discussed briefly where we came from and where we were going, shook hands and went our way. I can think of no other make of car which would engender such a friendly spontaneous reaction.

When travelling in Africa it is prudent to fill up the petrol tank when one can, as the prospect of being stranded in the bush without fuel must be avoided at all costs. This is especially important with an MG TC which has only an unpredictable warning light instead of a proper fuel gauge. Shortly after crossing the frontier between Rhodesia and South Africa I pulled up at a ramshackle building beside which stood one of those ancient petrol pumps which had two glass bowls each with a capacity of one gallon. To operate it, the attendant pumped the fuel by a hand pump into one of the bowls and then opened a valve to allow it to empty itself by gravity into the tank of the car. As it emptied itself he filled the second bowl in the same way and repeated the procedure. As I was paying him, a lanky fellow of about thirty sauntered over to me and asked in a heavy Afrikaans accent:

"Man, can you give me a lift to the next dorp"?

"I am afraid I can't, I'm overloaded with luggage as it is", I replied

"Yrr Man, you got a spare seat next to you".

I can't take any more weight with those tyres", I said

"Come on man, Its only down the road to the next place", he insisted

"No chance", I said and at the same time I unzipped my leather jacket to take my wallet out of the bush shirt pocket, deliberately opening the jacket wide to expose the gun belt. As soon as he saw the holster, he turned round abruptly and walked off. I breathed a sigh of relief and silently thanked the AA for their advice.

The rest of the journey to Cape Town was uneventful, just miles and miles of khaki coloured bush, but on the second day the effect of driving with the hood down made itself felt. Although I kept the windscreen up, the combination of heat and dust on my face turned the skin red and raw, so I pulled up at one of the small "General Stores" common in the less populated parts of Southern Africa and asked for some ointment to soothe the skin. The only cream available was a small blue tin of the ubiquitous Nivea Cream, which to my amazement and delight soothed the pain so quickly and effectively that I still use it today as an aftershave.

I timed the journey so that I would be in Cape Town about three hours before the boat left. I therefore drove straight to the port and as the cost of shipping the car was governed by the volume of the package, I set about reducing the overall height and width of the car to the declared minimum. This entailed folding the windscreen flat onto the bonnet, removing the mascot on the radiator cap, folding the roof down and covering the car with a fitted tonneau. The width was reduced by removing the wing mirror.

After dealing with the necessary paperwork I watched it being driven over a net and hoisted into the hold. With the car safely in bed, I walked up the gangway of what would be my home for the next two weeks.

By coincidence I shared the cabin with another aspiring engineer called Claude who was also travelling to England to finish his education. We spun a coin for the bottom bunk and I won, which proved to be a blessing. As we were both early boarders, we went back on deck and leaned on the railing watching the other passengers come on board. On the dockside, saying fond

MV Stirling Castle

good byes to their husbands, must have been at least two dozen young wives who were going home for holidays, weddings, anniversaries, whatever.

"Bye darling, give my love to Mummy."

"Don't forget to write."

"Love you darling."

These were the kind of final fond farewells called up to the departing spouses.

After the first dinner on board, my cabin mate and I perambulated round the upper decks to do some talent spotting, but if there were any, they had probably decided to have an early night. On the following evening the decks suddenly sprouted dozens of young, white-capped, gold-striped ship's officers who appeared like mushrooms from below, and soon all the single girls and young wives who boarded at Cape Town buzzed around them like bees around a honey pot. It was as if these women took their morals and inhibitions, wrapped them in water proof paper, tied them with a ribbon and threw them overboard. By ten o'clock they were all paired up, which left Claude and me bemoaning our misfortune. This, I decided, was going to be a lonely trip. You can't compete with a ship's officer, even if he is only a scrubbed up grease monkey from the engine room.

Two days later, I was sitting in a deck chair on the top deck reading Irving Stone's "Lust for Life", when I noticed a girl about my age promenading round the deck. On her second circuit she suddenly stopped in front of me, smiled and said:

"That's an intriguing title,"

"It's the story of Van Gogh" I said

"I love Van Gogh" she said, "Mind if I join you?"

I pulled the nearest deckchair a bit closer and beckoned her to sit down.

"What makes you brave the waves?" I asked

"I am visiting my aunt in London, and you?"

"I'm going back to finish my studies," I replied

"What sort of studies?"

"Engineering,"

"That doesn't sound very sexy," she said. This remark shook me a little

"Why does it have to be sexy?" I asked

"I like sexy men," she said. My God, I thought, this is too good to be true.

"Well, I'm a sexy engineer," I said

"I have never known a sexy engineer,"

"Come down to my cabin and you'll find they do exist"

"OK", she said and got up from her deck chair. Just like that.

Five minutes later we were on my bottom bunk making love and did so daily for the remainder of the passage. At Southampton we kissed good-bye and did not even bother to exchange addresses. The honeymoon was over. I came to the conclusion that there must be something about a sea voyage which turns women on. Whether it is the vibration of the engines or the realisation that they are cut off from the rest of the world, the fact remains that on this trip respectable unaccompanied wives as well as singe women behaved in a way that they would never even have contemplated in normal surroundings.

The ship stopped for a day in Las Palmas in the Canaries and Claude and I decided to see the sights. We hired an ancient Buick taxi for a few hours, whose driver seemed to have his finger permanently on the horn, to take us into town. We looked around the shops and visited the Cathedral where one could literally change money in the nave. Talking about moneylenders in the Temple!. Then we went up the tower in a lift which was in fact only a platform with a hole and a rope in the middle operated by a young boy. As the lift ascended one could scrape one's hand along the brick wall of the tower. When we came down again we asked the taxi driver, who spoke very little English, to show us a part of the island not normally visited by tourists. He nodded as if he understood, and drove us for about ten minutes through a quiet residential area until we reached a large mansion that looked like a museum. There he stopped and indicated by hand movements that we should go in. A flight of stone steps led to a large door which opened up into a huge hall with a grand staircase at the end opposite the entrance and two doors on each of the side walls. There was no one about and after waiting a few minutes, just as we were about to leave, a woman came down the stairs and said something in Spanish.

Claude said in English "No speak Spanish".

The woman gave us a knowing smile and without a word, threw open one of the doors and beckoned us to go in. In the room was a bed in which slept what looked like a girl in her late teens. Our entry had clearly woken her up, because she rubbed her eyes, and said something in Spanish in a tired, plaintive voice which could well have been:

"Oh, not again".

I tapped Claude on the shoulder and said quietly:

"Let's get the hell out of here, this is a bloody brothel."

We both smiled at the woman, shook our heads and made for the door.

Outside the taxi driver looked amazed at our quick return.

"Now take us back the the ship please," I said.

England again

A week later, on a drizzling depressing October morning we docked in Southampton. I could not help comparing the grey, sad-faced dockers with the cheerful chattering loading gang in sun drenched Cape Town. Well, I said to myself, in three years I'll be back in Africa.

When I reached the front of the queue for the custom examination the custom officer looked at my passport and without looking up asked; "Anything to declare?"

"A car and a gun," I said

He looked up sharply. "A gun?"

"Yes, an automatic" I said and laid the holster with the pistol on the counter.

"Is it loaded?" he asked

"Of course," I said

"Please unload it," he said rather sharply.

As I took out the magazine and as I flipped out the bullets a small crowd had gathered to watch.

"You can't bring this in without a permit, you know," he said, "We will hold it for eight weeks, and if you don't get permission from the police by then it will be confiscated."

I just nodded and passed the gun with the loose bullets over to him. He gave me a receipt for the gun, stamped the carnet for the car and informed me that I had to keep the car for three years if I wanted to save paying import duty, He showed no further interest in any other item I brought in and waved me through.

It took about an hour for the car to be winched out of the hold and deposited gently on the dockside. I then had to remove the tonneau, hinge up the windscreen, erect the hood, re-fit my Indian Chief mascot on the radiator cap, re-fit the wing mirror, load and strap up my suitcases, and I was ready to brave the road to London.

Mrs Keane welcomed me like a lost son. My cabin trunk containing all my heavy goods had been sent in advance and was already in the room I had occupied six years earlier.

The next morning I registered my presence at Rhodesia House and went to the police station in Ladbroke Grove to get permission to retrieve my gun.

"Can I help you" said the burly police Sergeant behind the reception desk

"I'd like to have a permit to import my gun which is held by the Customs in Southampton" I said

"What do you want a gun for" he asked. This floored me a little.

"Self protection" was the best answer I could think of.

"Where do you come from" he then asked

"Southern Rhodesia". He placed his fists on his hips

"No need for a gun here Sonny, you're in a civilised country now"

I realised there was no point arguing.

About a month after my arrival, I received a letter from HM Customs reminding me that unless I obtained permission to import the gun, it would be confiscated. Without a police permit to keep it here I arranged through Thomas Cook, at a cost greater than the purchase price of the gun, to have it returned to my father in Rhodesia. The bullets I donated to the Queen.

A few days later was the 23 October 1952, my 25th birthday and the 10th anniversary of the Battle of El-Alamein. I always remembered this battle because it was, for the Western Allies, the turning point of the war and prompted Winston Churchill to utter the famous words:

"This is not the beginning of the end, but it is perhaps the end of the beginning".

I can think of no more apposite phrase to close this chapter of my life.

Appendix

I often wondered what became of that painting of the "Boy with the Mouthorgan". Fifty years later while on a two week's holiday in Israel, I decided to look for it. I took a bus from Tel Aviv to Ramat Gan where Ludwig Schwerin lived and worked and where, l learnt from friends they had established an art gallery devoted purely to his paintings, prints and etchings. Although I had to learn Hebrew at Esslingen for religious reasons, by the time I visited its country of origin I had forgotten most of what I learnt. It was with some difficulty therefore that I managed to locate the art gallery only to find it closed. I must have looked pretty forlorn as I stood helpless and utterly frustrated in front of the locked door, because a kindly middle aged lady came up to me and asked me in English whether I needed some help. After I explained that I came all the way from England to visit the gallery, she gave me the name of the curator and because her house was quite near, suggested that I knock on her door and ask her to open the gallery up for me. It was a long shot, but after my long journey from Tel Aviv, I had to give it a try. Having been told which house to go to, I rang the door bell. The door was opened by a youngish woman who asked me something in Hebrew which I could not understand but could only mean: "What do you want?"

"Do you speak English?" I asked.

"Yes I do," she replied.

I told her that I badly wanted to visit the Schwerin Gallery because I believed that there might be a picture of me in the collection. I then told her my story that we were both from the same town in Germany and of how and when he painted me several times.

That clearly did the trick. She immediately agreed that my visit should not be wasted and promptly accompanied me back to the gallery, which she opened up for me.

"I can only give you about an hour," she said, "I have to go somewhere after that"

"You really are very kind, I shan't hold you up," I said.

I looked at all the sketches, landscapes and, of course, all the portraits, but alas, no picture of me, not even a sketch. I was clearly disappointed, but after thanking her again and offering her at least the entrance fee, which she vehemently refused to accept, I took the next bus back to Tel Aviv.

Then, a few years later a strange thing happened. In 1997 my younger son, Marc, who was studying medicine at the Royal Free Hospital in Hampstead visited a friend, another medical student, at his home in Heidelberg. There, at a party, he was introduced to another young medic called Günther Frank whose father, Josef Frank, amazingly, was the Bürgermeister of Buchen. This meeting was obviously reported by Günther to his father who shortly afterwards invited me and my wife to visit my home town to be present at the opening of an exhibition of paintings and etchings by their "local-boy-made-good", Ludwig Schwerin in honour of his 100th birthday. In my acceptance letter I told him that Schwerin had actually painted me playing a mouthorgan, but I had no idea where the painting "Boy with Mouthorgan" now was or who owned it. To my astonishment, a few days later I received a letter from the exhibition organiser Dr. Brosch, enclosing a photograph of the painting with a note saying that in 1936 it was presented by the Jewish community of Berlin to a Professor Mittwoch on his 60th birthday for services to the community. The note also stated that Prof. Mittwoch emigrated to England in 1939. My wife immediately looked up the name Mittwoch in the London telephone directory and found that there was indeed a person of that name in Hampstead. When she rang, the number was answered by Professor Mittwoch's daughter. My wife explained the reason for the call.

"Yes, I remember the picture," the lady said "but after my father's death, it was taken by my sister who is a psychiatrist in Jerusalem." She then gave my wife the address.

My wife then wrote to the sister and offered to buy the picture as a present for my 80th birthday, a rather rash proposition as the price of Ludwig Schwerin's paintings can be in four figures. However, the sister said she rather liked it and did not want to part with it, but would arrange for a professional photographer to make a colour photograph and would send it to us so that we could then have it enlarged. To end the story, which I related to numerous guests at dinner parties, my older son had it enlarged and printed on canvas for my birthday and it now hangs in our sitting room. A copy also adorns the sitting room wall of my good Buchener friends Walter and Mabel Jaegle, who were largely instrumental in having this part of my life story published together with an anthology of poems in German, the local vernacular and English by my mother..

The visit to Buchen to attend the Schwerin exhibition was the first of a number of visits at some of which I was asked to speak to members of the local council and pupils of the secondary school about my experiences in Nazi Germany and my life in England.

9 781915 787866